By the Wa~~ter's Edge~~

Ireland's Best Coastal Retreats

Top Places to Stay, Eat and Drink

Written by Bridget Hourican and Claire Ryan

Edited by Emily Hourican

The Authors | Biographies

Bridget Hourican

Bridget Hourican is literary editor for *The Dubliner* magazine, and also writes for publications including *The Irish Times*, *Image Magazine* and *The Gloss*. She has reviewed bars, restaurants, theatre and film for *Time Out Dublin* and *Time Out Brussels*. She grew up in Brussels, but lives in Dublin, and has spent every summer in Kerry for over 20 years.

Claire Ryan

Claire Ryan is a journalist, travel writer and documentary producer. She has written for *The Sunday Independent*, *The Irish Independent*, *The Sunday Tribune* and *The Dubliner*. Prior to that, she spent six years working in the Dublin hospitality industry with lengthy stints in Fitzers Dawson Street, La Stampa and L'Ecrivain. She grew up in Tipperary Town and lives in Dublin.

Design: Kevin Walsh

Additional photography: Joanne Murphy

Additional research:
Steve Wynne-Jones, Mark Kelly, Lián Sherriff and Niall Doyle

Published by Madison Publications Ltd,
3 Adelaide Street, Dun Laoghaire, Co Dublin, Ireland
Tel: 01 236 5800

Madison Publications are the publishers of *Who's Who in Ireland* and *Hospitality Ireland* magazine.

Publisher's dedication: To Anita with thanks

All rights reserved by Madison Publications Ltd. Reproduction without permission is strictly prohibited. Every care is taken in compiling the contents of this publication, but the proprietors assume no responsibility in the effects arising therefrom. Views expressed are not necessarily those of the proprietors.

© Madison Publications Ltd 2009
ISBN-978-0-9518728-9-5

By the Water's Edge | Welcome

Perhaps the best of Ireland is to be found beside the sea. Beautiful beaches, sheer cliffs, stark rocky outcrops, long stretches of jagged inlets – all the drama and wonder of the country are there in abundance. And these days there are also many excellent places to stay, eat and drink that take full advantage of the stunning natural backdrops. In celebration of these things, and in memory of many happy seaside holidays, we have produced *By the Water's Edge*, the first dedicated guide to Ireland's coastal regions.

Although there are some excellent guides to Ireland, if, like us, you are particularly inspired by the sea, you will already have encountered the frustration of trawling through various different books to get the information you need. Now, for the first time, all the essential details of the best coastal spots are gathered in one easy-to-read and attractive book. This book is intended to facilitate your trips to the sea, but also to trigger the desire to visit places you may never have heard of.

These are the most luxurious, picturesque and charming places with sea views from around the island of Ireland – where relevant, we have given you specific room numbers to request, for the best views. They amply demonstrate the ambition and talent of the many hoteliers, restaurateurs, chefs and publicans who devote themselves to meeting, and sometimes surpassing, our expectations, and we are proud to include them in this guide. However, because this is a book aimed at giving readers a clear picture of what awaits them, we have not pretended, as so many guidebooks do, that each and every one of them is perfect. Where there are shortcomings, we have pointed these out, and where extra praise is deserved, we have delivered that, too. Happily, we have found far more to praise than to criticise – a clear indication of the quality that now exists in this country.

I hope you will find this book both useful and inspiring; after all, as the old proverb goes: 'He that would learn to pray, let him go to sea.'

Emily Hourican
Editor

By the Water's Edge | Contents

History of the Irish Coastline	8
Ireland Map	10
Blue Flag Beaches	11

Leinster — 12

Dublin	13
Louth	23
Wexford	27
Wicklow	35

Munster — 40

Clare	41
Cork	53
Kerry	73

Connaught — 98

Galway	99
Mayo	115
Sligo	121

Ulster — 124

Antrim	125
Derry	131
Donegal	135
Down	145

A-Z Resorts Listing — 152

Resort listing symbols

Golf   Fishing   Good Food   Luxurious   Historical   Good Value

Ireland | A Coastal History

For muir gáirech, gairt in ruirich, Cechaing tonnaig, tresaig magain, mongaig rónaig, roluind mbedcaig, mbruichrich mbarrfind, faílid mbrónaig.
On the clamorous sea he called to the great king ...
He traversed the wavy tumultuous place, foaming, full of seals,
Very rough, leaping, turbulent, white-topped, joyful, sorrowful.

Early Irish poem, c. 650 AD

Antique map of Ireland, published by the Dutch cartographer Willem Blaeu in *Atlas Novus*, 1635

The early Irish understood the power of the sea. As farmers and fishermen, the lives of the early Irish settlers were governed by the waves that surrounded the country, inspired by the changing tides.

And it was from the sea, of course, that Ireland's history was shaped, with the legends of Gaelic culture over several centuries BC speaking of 'ancient invaders' and their influence. It's said that the fascinating Giant's Causeway on the County Antrim coast, was formed when Celtic hero Fionn Mac Cumhaill attempted to bridge the Irish Sea to fight his great Scottish rival, Benadonner.

St. Patrick, the patron saint of Ireland, is said to have brought Christianity to Irish shores in the early fifth century AD, but the noble prophet was just one in a series of influential arrivals from beyond the waves. The Vikings, in the eighth and ninth centuries, brought huge cultural influences, settling in locations such as Dublin and Waterford and developing them into the port towns they are today. The coming of the Normans two centuries later further impacted the early Gaels, and the invasion of King Henry II in 1171 is long thought to be the moment when Ireland lost its freedom to become part of the British Empire for the next 750 years.

One of Ireland's most notable coastal towns, Kinsale, County Cork, has an chequered history, chiefly as the scene of a battle in 1601

Charles Fort, in Kinsale, Co. Cork, built in the late seventeenth century

between Irish/Spanish and English forces, which ultimately led to the fleeing of the country by much of the Irish nobility, the 'Flight of the Earls'. The port was also, at one stage, one of the busiest in the UK and Ireland for wine imports – in the 18th century, Ireland was the biggest importer of the fine wines of Bordeaux in the world. It was said at the time that Ireland 'flowed with wine as much as the land of Caanan with milk.'

The plantations of the sixteenth and seventeenth centuries left native Ireland in an impoverished state, and it was out of this that Ireland's most significant – and tragic – relationship with the sea was born. The Great Famine of 1845 to 1852 saw millions of Irish take their chances aboard ships bound for the New World, never to return to Irish shores. It's estimated that between 1.5 and 2 million fled the country during this period.

The post-Famine years saw a resurgence in maritime interest, with the development of new fishing industries around the Cork-and-Kerry coast – developments that gave rise to major port and shipbuilding developments in the mid-to-late nineteenth century. Perhaps the most [in]famous cruise-liner of them all, Titanic, was built at the Harland and Wolff shipyard in Belfast, County Antrim – one of 70 such ships produced there for the famous White Star Line.

Remarkably, the twentieth century saw Ireland's relationship with the sea diminish slightly, as the now autonomous leaders of Ireland looked inward to the development of more internal industries. Ireland's fish stocks were decimated, and only in the past 20 years has the government put in place methods of recovery for what should be, but sadly isn't, one of the country's key industries.

It may stretch to over 7,500 km, but every yard of Ireland's coastline has an intrinsic link with Irish heritage and culture. After all, in what other country can you boast that you're never more than 100 kilometres from the nearest shore, wherever you are?

By the Water's Edge | Coastal Retreats | **9**

IRELAND | Map

Ireland | Blue Flag Beaches

What does a Blue Flag mean?

The Blue Flag is a voluntary eco-label that works towards sustainable development at beaches/marinas through strict criteria dealing with water quality, environmental education and information, environmental management and safety, and other services. Ireland has a total of 83 Blue Flags.

Co. Antrim
Portrush West Strand
Whiterocks

Co. Clare
Ballycuggeran
Cappa
Fanore
Kilkee
Mountshannon
White Strand Doonbeg
White Strand Miltown Malbay

Co. Cork
Barleycove
Garretstown
Garryvoe
Inchydoney
Owenahincha
The Warren (Rosscarbery)
Tragumna
Youghal Claycastle

Co. Derry
Portstewart Strand
Magilligan, Benone
Downhill

Co. Donegal
Bundoran
Carrickfinn
Culdaff
Fintra
Killahoey
Lisfannon
Marble Hill
Murvagh
Portnoo (Narin)
Portsalon
Rossnowlagh
Stroove

Co. Down
Cranfield West
Tyrella
Murlough

Co. Dublin
Dollymount
Killiney
Seapoint

Co. Galway
An Trá Mór (Inverin)
Ceibh An Spideal
Cill Muirbhthe (Aran)
Loughrea Bathing Place
Salthill
Silverstrand
Traught
Trá an Doilín

Co. Kerry
Ballinskelligs
Ballybunion North
Ballybunion South
Ballyheigue
Banna
Derrynane
Fenit
Inch
Kells
Maherabeg
Rossbeigh
Ventry
White Strand Cahirciveen

Co. Louth
Port Lurganboy
Shellinghill/Templetown

Co. Mayo
Bertra
Carrowmore
Clare Island
Dooega
Dugort
Elly Bay
Golden Strand
Keel
Keem
Mullaghroe
Mulranny
Old Head
Ross

Co. Sligo
Mullaghmore

Co. Waterford
Clonea Strand
Councillors Strand
Dunmore East

Co. Westmeath
Quigleys Marina Ltd

Co. Wexford
Courtown
Curracloe
Morriscastle
Rosslare
Kilmore Quay Marina (Blue Flag Marina)

Co. Wicklow
Brittas Bay North
Brittas Bay South

By the Water's Edge | Coastal Retreats | 11

Leinster

Leinster | Co. Dublin

County Dublin

Introduction

The beauty of Dublin has always been its location, bounded by the mountains on one side and the sea on the other. Much of the city's sweep is coastal, hugging the bay to north and south, with many areas of outstanding beauty along the way. A DART ride from Howth to Bray will show you most of these, and prove that Dublin's beaches, jetties, piers and breakwaters can rival anywhere in the country. But this is no static, picture-postcard beauty. Dublin Bay is still a busy, vibrant centre of economy, with working ports and 40 major ship movements daily. That said, relaxing with a pint or a good meal in any of the excellent seaside bars, restaurants or hotels, you could be forgiven for thinking otherwise.

By the Water's Edge | Coastal Retreats | 13

Leinster | Co. Dublin

Finnegan's
2 Sorrento Road, Dalkey, Co. Dublin
T: 01 285 8505 W: www.finnegans.ie
Opening Times: Year round
Directions: *[Map Ref. 1] Walking from DART to Dalkey Village, on right-hand side*

Bono's local looks very trad and old-school – all mahogany bar, oxblood walls, intimate snugs, and priestly stained-glass windows. It added an extension a few years ago, frequently a disastrous thing, but less disastrous here than elsewhere. Come to see Dalkey locals and celebs – George Clooney allegedly dropped in on Christmas Eve. Does a decent lunch (no dinners), with stalwarts like steamed mussels, stuffed pork and raspberry crumble.

Nosh €
111 Coliemore Road, Dalkey, Co. Dublin
T: 01 284 0888 W: www.nosh.ie
Opening Times: Year round
Directions: *[Map Ref. 2] DART end of Dalkey Village*

Devotees of this modern restaurant tend to be well-heeled social climbers, who never ever leave Dalkey (quelle horror!), but don't let that put you off. Even the would-be glitterati need their comfort food. Get in line, order the eggs Benedict (€13.50) off the brunch menu, or the beer-battered fish 'n' chips and mushy peas (€14.50 lunch, €20.95 dinner). Your conversation should be frivolous, gossipy and pitched low, to titillate and frustrate earwigging diners. Do not come here to break up or to talk about Serious World Issues.

The Queen's Bar and Restaurant € 🏠
Castle Street, Dalkey, Co. Dublin
T: 01 285 4569 W: www.thequeens.ie
Opening Times: Year round
Directions: *[Map Ref. 3] Centre of town*

Apparently one of the oldest pubs in Ireland, but the spruce, contemporary-meets-trad interior adds a welcome dash of modernity. This place serves families, chattering teens, tourists and the odd auld fellow, so turnover is fast (for food; you can nurse your pint as long as you like). Sit up at the bar and share chicken wings with blue cheese (€10.95) or steak and kidney pie (€10.25), or head into the restaurant where prices are slightly higher.

The Queen's Bar and Restaurant

Leinster | Co. Dublin

Leinster | Co. Dublin

Cavistons

59 Glasthule Road, Dun Laoghaire, Co. Dublin
T: 01 280 9245 **W:** www.cavistons.com
Opening Times: Year round
Directions: *[Map Ref. 4] Turn right at Sandycove DART station, towards Dalkey*

Glasthule is the culinary capital of South Dublin thanks to all those wine shops and butchers selling boar sausages, but mostly because of this place. Cavistons has been selling wild salmon, trussed pheasant and blue cheeses to yummy mummies for 50 years. About a decade ago it opened a lunch restaurant, and this spring it began opening for dinners at weekends. Cue Southside ecstasy. This is one of the few places where opening during a recession presents no risk. Only 28 seats, so book well in advance. Food not particularly cheap (€28 seared scallops), but usually delicious.

O'Loughlin's

26 Lower Georges Street, Dun Laoghaire, Co. Dublin
Opening Times: Year round
Directions: *[Map Ref. 5] Approx 50 yards from entrace to Bloomfield Shopping Centre, opposite post office*

This place is like a time-warp – stepping through the door, you're met with indifferent silence: no music, a few locals turning their heads to stare at you incuriously. Of course it has fanatical devotees, who won't thank us for giving it the oxygen of publicity and sending tourists its way. Arguably the best stout in the city. Not very keen on women – they're not banned outright, but there's no ladies' loo ... we can take a hint ...

Abbey Tavern

Abbey Street, Howth, Co. Dublin
T: 01 839 0307 **W:** www.abbeytavern.ie
Opening Times: Year round
Directions: *[Map Ref. 6] Centre of Howth, 50 yards from harbour*

Tourists flock to Howth, and especially to the Abbey Tavern, which dates back to the sixteenth century, looks olde worlde and does a traditional Irish night, with five-course dinner and music. Don't let that put you off having a pint, sandwich (€4.75) or fish 'n' chips (€14.95) for lunch. The turf fire is always roaring, the decor – flagged floors, stone walls – is a bit too authentic, but still cosy. Prices and quality at The Loft restaurant upstairs are also competitive: chowder €6, Clonakilty black pudding €7.50, and baked salmon €18.50.

Leinster | Co. Dublin

Aqua ⓧ
West Pier, Howth, Co. Dublin
T: 01 832 0690 W: www.aqua.ie
Opening Times: Year round
Directions: *[Map Ref. 7] End of west pier*

One of the best places to eat in Howth if you want a sea view, Aqua is at the end of the west pier, with views of Ireland's Eye from the floor-to-ceiling windows in its bright first-floor room. Food is simple and trad-modern with a twist. For starters, try the seared tuna with a gazpacho shot and wasabi cream (€13), then take the organic salmon with wild-mushroom risotto and fig dressing (€29). You won't get those on the early-bird menu, but then, at €30, the early bird is very recession-chic.

Ivan's Oyster Bar and Grill ⓧ
17-18 West Pier, Howth, Co. Dublin
T: 01 839 0285 W: www.ivans.ie
Opening Times: Restaurant closed Mon; early closing (8pm) Sun; oyster bar open daily from noon
Directions: *[Map Ref. 8] West Pier, to right of Howth DART station*

The latest jewel in the Beshoffs crown won Best New Restaurant 2008 from the Restaurants Association of Ireland and a sheaf of mouth-wateringly good reviews from just about every restaurant

Leinster | Co. Dublin

critic in the country. Not surprising – located on Howth's west pier, this airy, spacious room, with its big windows, benches running along the sides and large plants, manages to be both cool/minimalist and cheerful/welcoming (quite a trick). Chef Bogdan Danila is confident in his ingredients – fish is from the adjacent Beshoffs at the Market, and so fresh it's swimming. Try the native oysters (€18.50) – more expensive than the farmed variety, but worth it. The starters are imaginative – our favourite, the lobster cocktail (€14.50). Some of the mains are a bit busy – the hake with carrot and crab (€26) was overpowered by the citrus vierge sauce – but service is attentive, the house wine (€21) is light and refreshing, and the panna cotta (€7.50) lifts you up and rounds you off.

King Sitric ⊗

East Pier, Howth, Co. Dublin
T: 01 832 5235 **W:** www.kingsitric.ie
Opening Times: Year round
Directions: *[Map Ref. 9] Opposite east pier; 10-minute walk from DART*

You can't use your mobile in the dining room, which is either an excellent rule or unspeakable, depending on your demographic. Almost 40 years in business, the King Sitric (named for a Norse king) takes fine dining seriously. You order downstairs before being shown to the bright first-floor room, which is a bit old-school in decor, but has fantastic sea views. The à la carte is pricey (€52 for a large Dover sole), but for €58, you'll get a six-course dinner and attentive service. The eight bedrooms in the attached guesthouse have sea views and are clean, comfortable, elegant and quiet, but on the small side for the price (from €72.50pps).

Bon Appétit ⊗

9 St. James's Terrace, Malahide, Co. Dublin
T: 01 845 0314 **W:** www.bonappetit.ie
Opening Times: Closed first week Jan; first 2 weeks Aug
Directions: *[Map Ref. 10] Off Malahide Main Street; left turn after Church Road*

Don't let that forbidding Michelin star put you off – the set menu is €50, and for €25 extra, you can get the prestige menu, complete with sorbets, petits fours and amuses bouches (all the frills of

Opposite: Bon Appétit, Malahide

Leinster | Co. Dublin

Leinster | Co. Dublin

Michelin dining)! This is a good deal, but if it still sounds pricey, head downstairs for the brasserie, where starters like rock oysters are €8.50. However, the silk-walled, le Brocquy-printed, classically proportioned rooms overlooking Malahide Tennis Club are just the place to try ravioli of prawn, Parmesan polenta, and cherries in Riesling ...

Gibney's of Malahide
New Street, Malahide, Co. Dublin
T: 01 845 0606 W: www.gibneys.com
Opening Times: Year round
Directions: *[Map Ref. 11] Centre of Malahide Village; turn left at DART station, then left at traffic lights on main road*
This Malahide (and Dublin) institution has been going strong for five generations. By now a vast and cavernous place of, at the last count, seven bars and lounges, come the weekend, it's heaving with students, but is quieter midweek and does decent bar food (served till 8pm). The attached off-licence is one of the best in the country – over 700 wines – and for €6 corkage, you can drink any wine bought there with your meal.

Red Bank House and Restaurant
5-7 Church Street, Skerries, Co. Dublin
T: 01 849 1005 W: www.redbank.ie
Opening Times: Year round
Directions: *[Map Ref. 12] Skerries Town, opposite AIB*
You're here to golf or because it's a cute fishing village 20 minutes from Dublin Airport. Chef-proprietor Terry McCoy is passionate about quality and local produce, so the fish is from Skerries Harbour, and the flour in the home-made bread from local millers. It's pricey – €13 for garlic mushrooms! €42 for black sole! – and yes, the food is good, varied and adventurous, but perhaps not enough for these prices. B&B (from €50pps) in the comfortable, adjacent 18-room Red Bank guesthouse is better value and the breakfasts (scrambled eggs and smoked salmon) bring guests back.

Stoop Your Head
Harbour Road, Skerries, Co. Dublin
T: 01 849 2085
Opening Times: Lunch and dinner daily; Sun 4pm-8pm

Leinster | Co. Dublin

Howth harbour, Co Dublin

Directions: *[Map Ref. 13] On harbour in Skerries*
You'll probably have to wait for a seat (no bookings), but you'll be seated at the bar, given excellent Guinness, and invited to peruse the blackboard for the day's menu, or to gaze out over the harbour, just metres away. Plus, turnover iss fast. The simplicity and solidity of the decor (bare, stripped-down wooden tables) is matched by chef Andy Davies' food – hearty, tasty, with the emphasis on fish. Try the mussels (€8.95) or Dublin Bay prawns fried in garlic butter (€18.95). And they do a mean steak (€24.95).

By the Water's Edge | Coastal Retreats

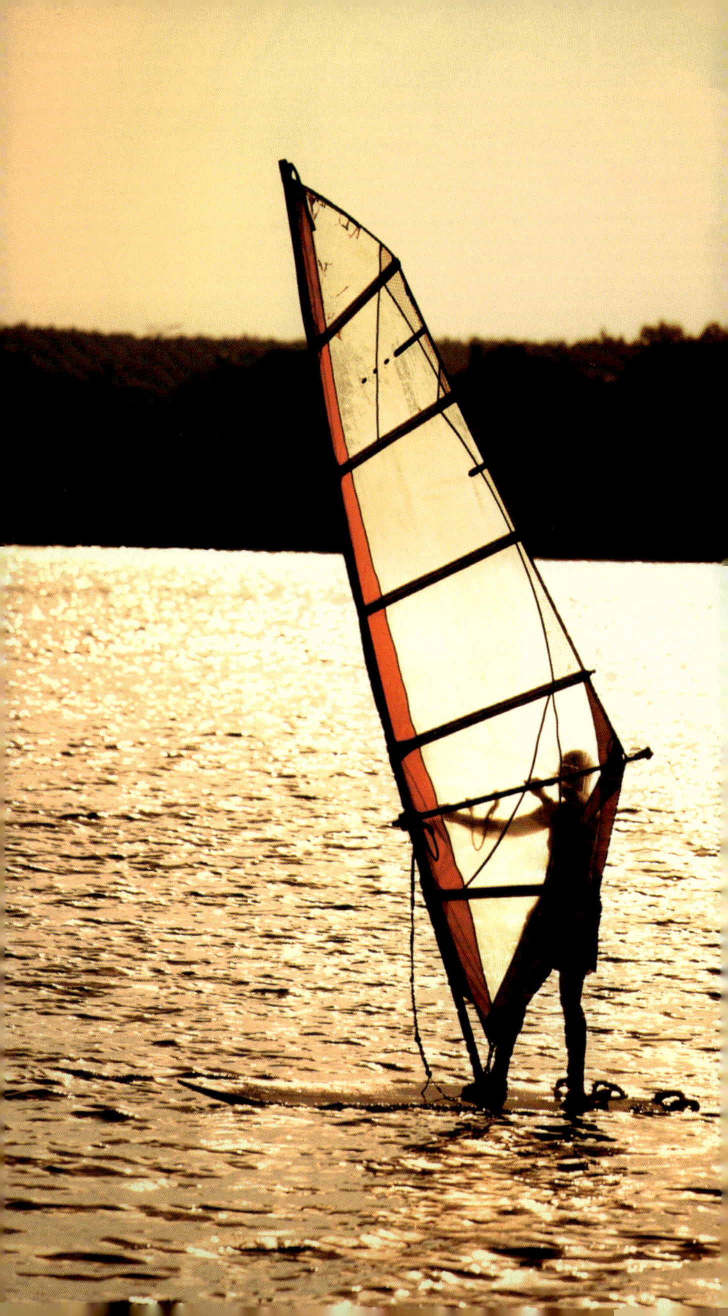

County Louth

Leinster | Co. Louth

Introduction
The coastline of the 'wee county' is just 70 kilometres long, but it is one of the most popular parts of Ireland for sailing, kitesurfing and angling. In the north, it connects with that of Northern Ireland at Carlingford Lough, and there are few experiences more pleasant than chartering a yacht from the Cooley Peninsula on a clear day and taking in the behemothic Mourne Mountains to the north. Coastal towns such as Clogherhead and Blackrock have developed as seaside resorts, taking advantage of Louth's sandy coastline, with the latter having appeared in a number of Hollywood films, including *Captain Lightfoot* and *The Devil's Own*.

Leinster | Co. Louth

Leinster | Co. Louth

Ghan House
Carlingford, Co. Louth
T: 042 937 3682 W: www.ghanhouse.com
Opening Times: 7pm; last orders, 9.30pm; Sunday lunch, 1pm-3.30pm
Directions: *[Map Ref. 1] Turn left (signposted) immediately after entering Carlingford Village from Dublin direction*
Ghan House is a beautiful Georgian house on Carlingford Lough with cookery school attached. It is warmly furnished with antiques – not five-star luxury, but relaxed period charm. The food, as you'd imagine, is generally very good and served in the atmospheric, candlelit dining room. However – the caveat – rooms in the annex are disappointing, small and functional. They are just not worth the €95pps. Prices in general are a bit high here, especially in 'the current economic climate'. We love Carlingford and we like Ghan House, but we think it could do with refurbishment and/or lowered prices. In the meantime: specify you want to stay in the main house (great sea/mountain views).

Kingfisher Bistro
Darcy McGee's Court, Dundalk Street, Carlingford, Co. Louth
T: 042 937 3716 W: www.kingfisherbistro.com
Opening Times: 11am-late
Directions: *[Map Ref. 2] Carlingford Town, off main road*
This locals' favourite reopened after renovations last year – it has now doubled its capacity (from a tiny 26 to an elegant sufficiency of 42), and is open for lunch and dinner seven days a week. Prices are still good, and the taste is still chef Mark Woods' trademark mix of trad (oven-baked salmon €18.95) meets the Orient (Thai-spiced pork €18.95). There's a good, small, varied wine list, and it all still works well.

Magees Bistro
Tholsel Street, Carlingford, Co. Louth
T: 042 937 3751 W: www.mageesbistro.com
Opening Times: Mon-Fri, 6.30pm-9.30pm; Sat-Sun, 6pm-10pm
Directions: *[Map Ref. 3] Near gate tower, across road from O'Hare's*
Magees' location alone would guarantee custom: on a paved street, by the gate tower, in the heart of medieval Carlingford, but the food

Opposite: Carlingford, Co. Louth

Leinster | Co. Louth

is tasty and good value. Decor is rather startlingly colourful but jolly, and you can see into the busy kitchen. Menus are short, sharp and traditional, with such classics as Caesar salads, oysters, seafood platter, fillet of beef and lobster. The pretty courtyard is a bonus for smokers.

Shalom

Ghan Road, Carlingford, Co. Louth
T: 042 937 3151 **W:** www.jackiewoods.com
Opening Times: Year round
Directions: *[Map Ref. 4] From south, take first right turn past Four Seasons Hotel, follow signs to gate; opposite sailing club*
One of your best bets for a room with a view of Carlingford Lough is Jackie Woods' B&B and self-catering apartments, five minutes' walk from the town. In the B&B, only the dining room overlooks the sea, but the modern, well-appointed self-catering apartments have front-facing balconies. B&B rooms are comfortable and functional, rather than luxurious, but the gardens are very pretty. The price is fine (€35-45pps), and Jackie is helpful and hospitable. Go for self-catering if you can get 'em; apartments (€90-115 per night) are spacious and private.

Kingfisher Bistro, Carlingford

Leinster | Co. Wexford

County Wexford

Introduction

Wexford, in the sunny south-east, has long been a tourist favourite, and with good reason. Rosslare has been proven the sunniest spot in Ireland, and the town is home to a Blue Flag beach. Along the coast, there are also beaches at Curracloe, Courtown and Duncannon. The Saltee Islands, which lie just five kilometres off Wexford's southern coast, form one of the country's largest bird sanctuaries, popular with bird-spotters and day-trippers alike. The little village of Kilmore Quay is an excellent spot to partake in some fishing or sailing, and draws a crowd to its seafood festival every summer. Further along the south coast, you will find the magnificent scenery at Ballyteigue Burrow. This nine-kilometre stretch of sand is a protected nature reserve, rich in wildflowers, wildlife and butterflies. It is also close to the historic Hook Head Lighthouse.

Leinster | Co. Wexford

Leinster | Co. Wexford

Dunbrody Country House Hotel
Arthurstown, Co. Wexford
T: 051 389 600 W: www.dunbrodyhouse.com
Opening Times: Closed 22-26 Dec
Directions: *[Map Ref. 1] R733 from Wexford to Arthurstown; signposted*

When 'eat local' and 'slow cooking' aficionado Kevin Dundon isn't on TV, he's here, presiding over this Georgian manor with his wife, Catherine. Located on Hook Peninsula, with views of Waterford City across the estuary, Dunbrody House enjoys a pretty spectacular setting. It also offers 20 acres of parkland and gardens to explore. The interior aims for comfortable luxury, with open fires, oak floors and plenty of antiques to give an ancestral feel. The modern world gets a nod also, with splashes of the contemporary, like the lavish Dundon's Champagne Seafood Bar and Terrace. Converted outbuildings house a spa and a cookery school, where Angelina and Brad learned how to bake brown bread – yes, really. However, staying here and emulating the A-listers will cost you – prices start at €135pps. Bedrooms and suites are fairly big, bathrooms are great, and the Molton Brown toiletries a thoughtful touch. The restaurant offers a 'Full-on Irish' tasting (€80) and set-menu deals (two-/three-course dinner €52/€65). An expensive but luxurious weekend away.

Glendine Country House
Arthurstown, Co. Wexford
T: 051 389 500 W: www.glendinehouse.com
Opening Times: Year round
Directions: *[Map Ref. 2] R733 to Arthurstown; on right before village*

Located on Hook Peninsula, this pretty farmhouse has stunning views across the Barrow Estuary. The six en suite bedrooms are called after local castles. All are very large, with good sea views. Request the Kings Bay Suite for the best view of the water (B&B €65pps). In terms of decor, think bright pine and heavy oak furniture, lightened by lovely floral soft furnishings and a smattering of antiques. The kids will love the Highland cows, horses and sheep, which they can feed if they ask nicely, and there is a safe playground beside the house. Breakfast is hearty and

Opposite: Dunbrody Country House Hotel

Leinster | Co. Wexford

Glendine Country House, Arthurstown, Co. Wexford

varied, from stewed rhubarb or smoked salmon and eggs to the full Irish. Dinner available (three courses €49), but be sure to pre-book.

Marsh Mere Lodge
Arthurstown, Co. Wexford
T: 051 389 186 W: www.marshmerelodge.com
Opening Times: Year round
Directions: *[Map Ref. 3] 100 miles from Dublin or Cork; 30 miles from Rosslare Harbour ferry*
This cosy and welcoming B&B offers gorgeous views over Kings Bay and the Hook Head lighthouse. There are four en suite rooms (B&B €50pps). All are brightly and handsomely decorated with solid antique dressing tables and large mahogany beds. Rooms are not terribly big, but lovely. They don't have views of the water, but you will find that particular aspect from the veranda or the gallery sitting room, where you can watch the sun set over the sea. You'll

Leinster | Co. Wexford

also find the bread freshly baked and the eggs recently laid by the hens roaming free. Breakfast is cooked to order, with eggs any way you like.

Castleview Heights Restaurant

Our Lady's Island, Broadway, Co. Wexford
T: 053 913 1140
Opening Times: Closed Mon-Tue off-season
Directions: *[Map Ref. 4] N25 to Rosslare, turn right after Tagoat, signs to Our Lady's Island; 300 metres on right after village*

A good reason to stretch the legs en route to Rosslare. Take time to appreciate views over the castle ruins and the inlet around Our Lady's Island, a pilgrimage hotspot. This restaurant has a country-cafe-style interior, with patio seating available outside. No frills, but the view makes up for any lack thereof. It's unpretentious and friendly. Family-orientated facilities. A craft shop, 18-hole par-3 golf course, and, in good weather, a trampoline and bouncing castle will allow you a few minutes' peace to enjoy a bowl of mussels or calamari before gathering the troops. Sunday set lunch €20.

Kilmokea Country Manor

Great Island, Campile, Co. Wexford
T: 051 388 109 **W:** www.kilmokea.com
Opening Times: Year round
Directions: *[Map Ref. 5] N733 from New Ross to Ballyhack, follow signs for Kilmokea Gardens*

Think Agatha Christie; this country manor is quaint, polite and rather English, from its Georgian tea room to the bread-baking and jam-making. The house is a charming old rectory that sits on seven acres of heritage gardens. Proximity to the coastline means deep-sea fishing a short drive away, as well as plenty of beaches and quaint fishing villages to explore. They have recently opened an indoor swimming pool, sauna and jacuzzi. Be warned: there is a charge to use the latter (€20 per half-hour). For the nicest views over the gardens, stay in the lovely Magnolia Room, with its four-poster bed (B&B €150pps), or the Rose Room (B&B €125pps). Dinner is served in the Peacock dining room (two/three courses €48/€54). Self-catering accommodation is also available.

Leinster | Co. Wexford

The Lobster Pot ⓧ
Ballyfane, Carne, Co. Wexford
T: 053 913 1110
Opening Times: Closed Mon (excluding bank holidays) and first five weeks of year; no reservations in high season (Jun-Aug) or bank-holiday weekends.
Directions: *[Map Ref. 6] 5 kilometres from Rosslare; follow signs for Carnsore Point*

If you like your fish freshly caught, relaxed surroundings and a well-pulled pint, try the Lobster Pot. Its cosy green colour and interconnecting rooms gives it a real cottage feel. This country pub is anchored in rural hospitality and serves its locally sourced seafood simply and well. Service is attentive and the menu extensive. Try the chowder (€8.75), River Rush oysters (€11.95) or the house speciality, baked crab mornay (€13.95). There is also plenty of choice for non-fish fans: steak, lamb, chicken or duck. Standards are above average for a pub. Popular with locals and tourists alike, the Lobster Pot tends to fill up very quickly.

Aldridge Lodge ⓧ
Duncannon, New Ross, Co. Wexford
T: 051 389 116 W: www.aldridgelodge.com
Opening Times: Dinner served Wed-Sat, 7pm-9.30pm; Sunday dinner sittings, 5.30pm and 8.30pm
Directions: *[Map Ref. 7] 200 metres outside Duncannon, overlooking beach*

Don't be fooled by this dormer house. Behind the rather ordinary facade is a touch of class. From its elevated view over Duncannon fishing village, to its elegant decor and first-rate food, everything about this place is above the ordinary. The light-filled, award-winning restaurant spills onto a deck with stunning sea views. Try the Hook Head crab claws, but don't stop there. The set menu is a delicious steal at €38.50 – and you don't have to leave after dinner. Stay in one of the three en suite rooms. Room 1 has fantastic views of Duncannon Beach (B&B €55pps).

Sqigl Restaurant and Roches Bar ⓧ €
Quay Road, Duncannon, New Ross, Co. Wexford
T: 051 389 188 W: www.sqiglrestaurant.com
Opening Times: Dinner from 7pm, Tue-Sat; bar food served daily, 12.30pm-6pm; closed Jan

Leinster | Co. Wexford

Kelly's Resort Hotel and Spa, Rosslare

Directions: *[Map Ref. 8] Village centre*
Part old-man pub, part barn conversion and modern Irish restaurant, this double-sided gem is located in the heart of Duncannon Village and across from a Blue Flag beach. On a lovely Wexford day, sit in Roches' beer garden to sample bar food that includes open sandwiches and hot daily specials. The trendy offspring, Sqigl Restaurant, is run by the proprietor's daughter. Though intimate – it only seats 36 – the room still manages to feel bright, airy and modern. Good-value set dinner menu (€42.50). Lots of quality local seafood. Service is warm and efficient.

Kelly's Resort Hotel and Spa

Rosslare, Co. Wexford
T: 053 913 2114 W: www.kellys.ie
Opening Times: Year round
Directions: *[Map Ref. 9] 20 kilometres from Wexford Town; along Rosslare Strand*
Regulars love this place like family; given the terrific amenities, beautiful beachside location and spectacular sea views, we can see why. Some rooms need updating, but there is great food and value to be found here. Beaches, the more formal of the two restaurants, offers decent set-menu options (three-course lunch €25; dinner €50). La Marine is the funkier sister restaurant with a bistro feel. Think goat's cheese crostini (€18.50) and Wexford rib-eye (€18.95).

By the Water's Edge | Coastal Retreats | 33

Leinster | Co. Wexford

This is a destination hotel, and its leisure facilities will keep you occupied. There are two indoor swimming pools, a gym, a 'SeaSpa', indoor tennis and croquet to be enjoyed. The outdoors should be explored, too. Fishing and golf can be easily arranged nearby. The huge art collection will thrill you, as will the 360-degree view of the sea from the O' Malley Suite (€180pps, includes dinner and B&B) – if you can afford it. Kelly's is child-friendly, with a supervised crèche, playroom and playground on site – beware of the 10 per cent surcharge on rooms. On the plus side, genial proprietor Bill Kelly has the finest collection of Châteauneuf du Pape for sale in the country, and service is consistently warm and friendly.

Heavens Above/The Sky and the Ground €

112 South Main Street, Wexford
T: 053 912 1273 **W:** www.wineanddinewexford.com
Opening Times: Year round
Directions: *[Map Ref. 10]* Town centre

You don't have to be religious to enjoy this three-level joint, but you will need to like candles and music. There are trad sessions five nights a week in the Sky and the Ground bar, and low lighting aplenty in the restaurant, Heavens Above, which has a worn, wooden look, with old advertisements dotted around the walls, and serves mid-range food to happy locals. Try the tempura of king prawn (€9.95) and the monkfish (€22.95). On the ground floor you'll find a good wine shop and bistro with tapas and a casual vibe (tapas platters for two €12.95). Friendly, easygoing, pub-like atmosphere on all levels.

Hook Head, Co. Wexford

County Wicklow

Introduction

Wicklow, known as 'the garden of Ireland', is renowned for its beautiful scenic views. The county is a mix of rolling hills, sandy coastline, woods and lakes. One of the best-known attractions, the sixth-century monastic centre at Glendalough, is located in the centre of the county, near the town of Laragh. The site is steeped in history, and its two great lakes are nestled in an imposing valley. Wicklow is packed with hidden gems, and has an abundance of magnificent houses and gardens, such as Kilruddery, Russborough and Powerscourt, the latter housing a Gordon Ramsay-signature restaurant at the Ritz-Carlton. The rugged landscape is the perfect setting for outdoor pursuits, such as angling, hillwalking, golf and horse-riding. Moving down the coast, the beach at Brittas Bay is a popular swimming spot. The main towns of Bray, Wicklow and Arklow all lie along the east coast.

Leinster | Co. Wicklow

Seafront at Bray, Co. Wicklow

Plattenstown House
Coolgreaney Road, Arklow, Co. Wicklow
T: 040 237 822
Opening Times: N/A
Directions: *[Map Ref. 1] Top of Arklow Town, small roundabout, straight on to Coolgreaney Road; 5 kilometres on left*

You'll find this period-farmhouse sanctuary 2.5 kilometres outside Arklow. Get some wild Wicklow air in your lungs by exploring the two acres of mature gardens and 50 acres of farmland. The four bedrooms (B&B €40pps) are pretty large and all overlook the gardens, but have showers that restrict the elbows slightly. This guesthouse is run with obvious pride and is packed with family heirlooms. Evening meals can be arranged if you don't fancy a night out in Arklow. A little worn round the edges, but the shabby-chic interior adds charm and colour, like the vicar's daughter in a Maeve Binchy novel.

Leinster | Co. Wicklow

Backstage@Bel's €
Church Road, Greystones, Co. Wicklow
T: 01 201 6990 W: www.bels.ie
Opening Times: Closed Mon
Directions: *[Map Ref. 2] Town centre*
The theatre theme is rather irrelevant, the good-value set menus aren't. Chef Jeff Norman, formerly of Roly's Bistro, here in partnership with his wife and mother-in-law, does the cooking and he does it well. Think classic dishes like fillet of Wicklow beef (€29) together with easygoing fare, like crispy ale-battered haddock (€19). Try to get a table by the huge windows that illuminate its clean, soft-cream, modern interior. The heated terrace at the front of the restaurant is a good opportunity to breathe in the salty Greystones air and watch the locals go by. Good pre-theatre menu (two courses €19.95; three courses €23.95).

Diva Restaurant and Piano Bar €
Greystones Harbour, Co. Wicklow
T: 01 201 7151 W: www.divarestaurant.ie
Opening Times: Dinner Mon-Fri; Sat-Sun, noon-close
Directions: *[Map Ref. 3] Over Beach House pub*
This is a local crowd-pleaser, and is Diva in name only. The family-friendly policy and extroverted Italian welcome makes it very popular with Greystones locals. Inside this busy restaurant you'll find a low-lit interior, stone walls and wooden beams. It's particularly inviting in winter, when roaring fires greet you. Great harbourside location marred momentarily by the construction of a new marina. Very extensive menu of pizza and pasta (€14.95), and fish and meat dishes (€18.95-28.95). A live pianist plays at the weekends while you eat, which you will either love or loathe. Crooners thrive here and have been known to grab the mike. You have been warned.

The Hungry Monk €
Church Road, Greystones, Co. Wicklow
T: (Restaurant) 01 287 5759; (Bistro) 01 201 0710
W: www.thehungrymonk.ie
Opening Times: Wed-Sat 6pm-11pm, Sun 12.30pm-7.30pm; bistro open Mon-Sat 5pm-11pm; lunch, Fri-Sat noon-3pm, Sun noon-10pm
Directions: *[Map Ref. 4] Greystones Village, beside DART*
The Hungry Monk doesn't need to adjust to the recession, just as it

Leinster | Co. Wicklow

never got too excited about the Tiger. It treats those two impostors – Triumph and Disaster – just the same. This stalwart doesn't open Monday or Tuesday and doesn't do weekday lunches (for lunch or Monday/Tuesday dinner, go downstairs to the Hungry Monk Wine-Bar Bistro for informal bar nosh, like burgers and scampi 'n' chips). The menu remains well priced and beautifully old-fashioned: lamb kidneys Dijonnaise (€8) and wild venison (€25). The fish menu depends on the catch, and Pat Keown is a vintner, so let him guide you through the wine list.

The Three Q's

Church Road, Greystones, Co. Wicklow
T: 01 287 5477
Opening Times: Closed Mon
Directions: *[Map Ref. 5] Main Street, beside DART station*
Run by the three brothers Quinn, the Three Q's may be small (just 30 seats indoors and eight outdoors), but it thinks big. This is a stylish joint, and behind the shopfront exterior peeps a little city sophisticate of a restaurant, with split-level seating. You can't see the sea, but it's there. Check out the nautical touch, with the porthole that looks into the kitchen. Fight for a table at brunch and try the corn fritters and pancetta (€7.95) with home-cut chips (€3.95) and home-made tomato sauce. Dinner is a smarter affair. Try the Wicklow venison pie (€20.95).

Below: Greystones, Co. Wicklow Opposite: Lifebuoy at Brittas Bay

Leinster | Co. Wicklow

Munster

Munster | Co. Clare

County Clare

Introduction

The many beauties of Clare are both evident and accessible. This jewel of the West Coast, bounded by the Shannon on one side and the Atlantic on the other, has drama, magic and pockets of endearing prettiness. The natural wonder of the Cliffs of Moher, with white water churning far below and thousands of seabirds calling, are about as breathtaking a sight as you'll see, and worth a considerable detour. Sometimes overlooked due to their billing alongside the Cliffs of Moher, the Bridges of Ross were once town bridges at the entrance to an inlet, until the ocean wore away the land around them. Clare has plenty of Blue Flag beaches: Cappa Pier, Kilkee, White Strand, Lahinch and Fanore. This is surfer territory, meaning frequently huge waves and a strong, welcome lifeguard presence.

By the Water's Edge | Coastal Retreats | 41

Munster | Co. Clare

The natural wonder of the Cliffs of Moher

An Fulacht Fia
Ballyvaughan, The Burren, Co. Clare
T: 065 707 7300 **W:** www.anfulachtfia.com
Opening Times: Year round
Directions: *[Map Ref. 1] Outside Ballyvaughan Village on coast road to Fanore*

Local man John Console built An Fulacht Fia ('the cooking pit') to take advantage of the views across Galway Bay. The wonderful garden, where you can sit out in good weather, is full of Burren plants. Inside it's contemporary but super-comfortable, rather than austerely minimalist – velvet seats, linen tablecloths, heavy curtains. Noise is never a problem here. The menu uses lamb, wild mushrooms, cider and other robust ingredients to great effect. Also excellent vegetarian options. Prices are West Coast average (starters about €9, mains about €25), but the early bird menu is €29.50.

Burren Coast Hotel
Ballyvaughan, The Burren, Co. Clare
T: 065 708 3000 **W:** www.burrencoast.ie

Munster | Co. Clare

Opening Times: Year round
Directions: *[Map Ref. 2] Ballyvaughan, beside pier and Monks pub*
A decent, mid-priced option for exploring the Burren with views of Galway Bay, the Burren Coast Hotel is part of the Atlantis Group, which also owns Tír gan Éan and Ballyvara House in Doolin. It recently added the Halcyon Spa, to get its fourth star. The rooms are not as chic as those in Tír gan Éan, but are still pleasant, comfortable and spacious (B&B €55-95pps). The Hazelwood Restaurant does decent food a tad below the usual West Coast prices (starters €9, mains €22). It's fairly new – 2007 – and had a few teething problems, but is shaping up well in reliable hands.

Gregans Castle Hotel

Ballyvaughan, The Burren, Co. Clare
T: 065 707 7005 W: www.gregans.ie
Opening Times: Closed Dec to mid-Feb
Directions: *[Map Ref. 3] On N67, 3.5 miles south of Ballyvaughan*
It's in the Burren – a fine eighteenth-century manor with its own landscaped gardens and chicly antique decor – but Gregans' biggest selling point is probably the food. Head chef Mickael Viljanen is confident, subtle, daring and light of hand. The ingredients are rich: lobster, quail's eggs, scallops, foie gras, etc., but you never feel stuffed or greedy (six-course dinner €65, nine-course tasting menu €80). Gregans was apparently a castle about ten centuries ago, but now looks like a handsome Georgian manor. There are no TVs in the rooms – the emphasis is on a quiet retreat. You'll find many retired couples, but this is also a good spot for a romantic weekend. From €97-225pps. Ask for the Galway Bay or Cappanawalla suites for sea views.

Aran View House Hotel

Doolin, Co. Clare
T: 065 707 4420 W: www.aranview.com
Opening Times: Easter-end Oct
Directions: *[Map Ref. 4] Edge of Doolin Town*
The name gives it away – you can see the Aran Islands. There may be more comfortable places to stay in Doolin, but none with a better view than this hilltop, family-run hotel on the edge of town. Make sure you get a room facing the Atlantic (ask for a suite) or you'll feel cheated, and do make allowances for some of the decor. B&B €55-70pps.

Munster | Co. Clare

Gregans Castle Hotel, Ballyvaughan

Ballinalacken Castle Country House
Doolin, Co. Clare
T: 065 707 4025 W: www.ballinalackencastle.com
Opening Times: Closed Nov to mid-Apr; restaurant closed Tue
Directions: *[Map Ref. 5] On R477, 2 miles from Doolin, 3 miles from Lisdoonvarna*
This luxury country house scores on service, atmosphere and location. Declan O'Callaghan, his wife, Cecilia, and father, Denis, are excellent hosts. The house was built in 1840 for Lord O'Brien and there are only 12 bedrooms. All are well renovated, with views of the sea or the fifteenth-century tower. Prices are competitive (€65-95pps). The restaurant in the opulent dining room (open to non-residents) is run by Michael Foley, previously of Dromoland Castle, who oversees its confident, adventurous menu: terrine of guinea fowl with pine nuts, Clare lamb coated in poppy seeds. Starters around €9.50, mains €27. A luxurious, quiet place from which to sally forth to the Cliffs of Moher and Doolin's pubs.

Munster | Co. Clare

Cullinan's Restaurant and Guesthouse
Doolin, Co. Clare
T: 065 707 4183 W: www.cullinansdoolin.com
Opening Times: Closed Christmas
Directions: *[Map Ref. 6] Centre of Doolin*
This small, bright restaurant by the Aille River does good things with local produce. The menu is concise, with a few fish dishes, lamb and beef. Try the crabmeat with lemon grass for starters (€12), then the John Dory with pancetta (€27). Excellent desserts – chocolate with caramelised walnut and caraway ice cream (€8). Early bird menu €30. The rooms above the restaurant are comfortable and reasonable value (€35-50pps), and you can get an omelette for breakfast. Nearby are the Cliffs of Moher and Doolin's pubs.

The Doolin Café €
Roadford, Doolin, Co. Clare
T: 065 707 4795 W: www.thedoolincafe.com
Opening Times: 10am-9pm daily in summer
Directions: *[Map Ref. 7] Roadford, centre of Doolin*
Deirdre Clancy and Niall Sheehy's simple cafe, with bare stone walls and ethnic art, is a favourite with backpackers, locals and tourists. After leasing it out for two years, they've returned, offering a simplified menu: soups (€3.95-4.50), salads, like broccoli and smoked bacon or Thai noodle (€7.95), and cakes (€3.75). Everything is home-made and very good. Sadly, no more full Irish breakfasts. They also sell books and CDs (the place resembles a cosy bookshop with cafe attached).

Gus O'Connor's €
Fisher Street, Doolin, Co. Clare
T: 065 707 4168 W: www.oconnorspubdoolin.com
Opening Times: Year round; kitchen closes 9pm
Directions: *[Map Ref. 8] Centre of Doolin*
People come to Doolin for the music, the set-dancing and because it's close to the Cliffs of Moher. Some of them complain that it's touristic, but if you can find a way to make a World Heritage Site not touristic, please tell us. Most visitors end up in Gus O'Connor's. Is it better than McDermott's or McGann's? Each has its (strident) champions. Visit all three and make an informed decision. O'Connor's has bar food (chowder €6.50, mussels €12.50) and

Munster | Co. Clare

nightly sessions finishing late. Music is more important than food here, so if you like quiet dining, go elsewhere.

Tír gan Éan

Doolin, Co. Clare
T: 065 707 5726 W: www.tirganean.ie
Opening Times: Mar-Oct
Directions: *[Map Ref. 9] Entering Doolin from Liscannor, turn right at crossroads*

It looks unassuming from the outside and there's no particular view, but inside, Tír gan Éan is classy and chic – its self-styling as a boutique hotel isn't misplaced. Plus, the staff are lovely. Bedrooms are in discreet muted shades, with crisp white sheets and flat-screen TVs, and underfloor heating in the bathrooms. Very good value at €60-80pps. The restaurant isn't always open – specify if you want to eat there when booking – but there's bar food all day and great breakfasts guaranteed.

The Lodge at Doonbeg

Doonbeg, Co. Clare
T: 065 905 5600 W: www.doonbeggolfclub.com
Opening Times: Year round
Directions: *[Map Ref. 10] 10 miles north of Kilkee*

This one's for special occasions – honeymoons or celebrating a film deal. Some of the most luxurious accommodation in Ireland, with some of the most stunning views. You don't have to be a golfer to enjoy it, although golfers will be in seventh heaven. Of the 69 suites/rooms, 18 have sea views, but the others look out on the river or the links – there are no bad views and no bad suites. Like all the best luxury places, it's the details that get people: Burren Perfumery products in the bathrooms, beds with eight plump pillows, and fresh flowers. Manager Bernie Merry ensures that everything runs like a Swiss clock. The spa has stone bathtubs and offers caviar facials. You have the choice of three places in which to dine: from 'simple' food in Darby's Bar to fine dining in the Long Room. The only possible complaint is that a sepulchral calm can descend on the dining room off-season – The Lodge is relatively newly opened to guests, and word is still getting around. You can get a one-bedroom deluxe for €160. The most expensive suite is €1,199 in high season, but that's for a four-bedroom suite that sleeps eight.

Munster | Co. Clare

The Lodge at Doonbeg

Stella Maris Hotel 🌍 💧
O'Connell Street, Kilkee, Co. Clare
T: 065 905 6455 W: www.stellamarishotel.com
Opening Times: Year round
Directions: *[Map Ref. 11] Centre of Kilkee, just past town square, overlooking bay*

Ann and Martin Haugh's jolly, red Victorian hotel in the centre of town and overlooking Kilkee Bay, is warm, friendly and welcoming to children and pets. This means it can be a bit noisy, but (for most) the laid-back but attentive service makes up for it. Rooms have been recently renovated, and although still functional rather than luxurious, most have huge beds and all have Egyptian cotton sheets. Ask for rooms 3 or 15-20 for ocean views. Summer rates are €70-80pps, winter rates €55-60pps. Unusually for a West of Ireland hotel, the Stella Maris is open all year round. Food served in the bar and restaurant is hearty, locally sourced and decent (though not especially refined). They'll arrange not just fishing, but dolphin-watching trips from Carrigaholt Village.

Munster | Co. Clare

Strand Restaurant and Guesthouse
Kilkee, Co. Clare
T: 065 905 6177 W: www.clareguesthouse.com
Opening Times: Mar-Dec
Directions: *[Map Ref. 12] Kilkee, on waterfront*
You get an amazing view of Kilkee Bay from the restaurant and some of the rooms, and windows in the restaurant are floor to ceiling, to take full advantage. The Strand has been serving food for over 160 years – to Percy French, Richard Harris and Russell Crowe, among others – and most of that time by the same family. Johnny and Caroline Redmond bought it a decade ago and offer a short, varied, intelligent menu, though perhaps a bit heavy on the cream. Service is very good. A new brasserie serving bar food is opening this spring – a welcome and recession-friendly development. Rooms upstairs are clean, comfortable and reasonable value (from €39pps), while a guest lounge facing the ocean is a bonus.

Barrtra Seafood Restaurant
Lahinch, Co. Clare
T: 065 708 1280 W: www.barrtra.com
Opening Times: Closed Jan-Feb, open daily Jul-Aug, varied opening hours other months (phone to enquire)
Directions: *[Map Ref. 13] 3.5 kilometres south of Lahinch on Miltown Malbay road*
This simple white building looking out on Liscannor Bay does great seafood at good prices. The dishes are quite old-fashioned – crab with avocado, honeydew melon, pepper steak, sticky toffee pudding – so there's a nostalgia factor to eating here. The early bird menu is €25 and the seafood menu is €38, which, on the West Coast, rates as excellent value. Theresa O'Brien is a good, old-school cook, and husband Paul an excellent host.

The Cornerstone
Main Street, Lahinch, Co. Clare
T: 065 708 1277
Opening Times: Year round
Directions: *[Map Ref. 14] Main Street, Lahinch*
Lahinch attracts golfers, so it has upmarket guesthouses and hotels. It also attracts surfers, so it offers a chilled vibe as well. If you want to encounter someone who has just caught The Wave,

Munster | Co. Clare

The view of Liscannor Bay, as seen from Barrtra Seafood Restaurant

golfers rueing 'the approach to the last' at the nearby Lahinch golf course, or locals watching the match, come to the Cornerstone and avail of its very excellent fish and chips, steaks or beef stew. It's always packed, so enjoy a pint while you wait. Trad sessions every Sunday and also on Thursdays and Fridays in summer.

Moy House

Lahinch, Co. Clare
T: 065 708 2800 W: www.moyhouse.com
Opening Times: Closed Jan
Directions: *[Map Ref. 15] On Miltown Malbay road outside Lahinch*
The classical elegance of this dazzlingly white eighteenth-century house, perched on Lahinch Bay, is borne out by the interior: antiques in an impeccably renovated setting – understated, tasteful luxury with an emphasis on comfort. Just nine rooms, the majority of which have sea views. Ask for the Well Suite if you're in the mood for luxury – it has a separate lounge with ocean views and a free-standing bathtub. B&B €92.50-180pps. Dinner is for residents only, and food is of the rich, country-house variety: foie gras, shellfish ravioli, suckling pig (set menu €55). Book ahead because dinner is

Munster | Co. Clare

Moy House, Lahinch

not always available. Service is exceptional – staff really can't do enough. Moy House has legions of devotees, so book well in advance.

Vaughan Lodge

Ennistymon Road, Lahinch, Co. Clare
T: 065 708 1111 W: www.vaughanlodge.ie
Opening Times: Closed Nov-Mar
Directions: *[Map Ref. 16] At edge of Lahinch, on left*
The golf course is half a mile away, the Cliffs of Moher 15 minutes' drive, and Liscannor Bay can be seen from the restaurant and some of the rooms – Vaughan Lodge has a great location. It also has exceptional service. The Vaughan family has run hotels in Clare since 1850, and Michael, Maria and son Daniel have the right blend of friendliness, professionalism and attention to detail. The lodge's rather uninspiring yellow exterior houses comfortable, well-planned rooms. It's purpose-built – all 22 bedrooms are large and well furnished. Half of them (the even numbers) have sea views. B&B €60-120pps. The food is seriously good, and the restaurant is famous in its own right. Chef Carol O'Brien trained in Dromoland

Munster | Co. Clare

and Gregans castles and produces traditional fare (Angus beef, scallops, monkfish), with a few surprises (guinea fowl, lamb with chestnut purée). Prices are West Coast average, which means not particularly cheap (average starter €9, mains €26), but in this case, merited.

Vaughans Anchor Inn
Liscannor, Co. Clare
T: 065 708 1548 W: www.vaughans.ie
Opening Times: Year round
Directions: *[Map Ref. 17] 4 kilometres from Lahinch on Cliffs of Moher road*

Vaughans Anchor Inn is very popular and packs them in. It doesn't take bookings, so get there early and keep your wits about you and your eye on your waitress. There's a reason for this popularity: good food that goes beyond the chowder/steamed mussels/crab claws of other seaside pubs. Although he does produce those perennial favourites, Denis Vaughan also branches out to foie gras, ravioli of lobster and pepper stuffed with monkfish. His prices, while above bar-food prices in general, are a bit below the restaurant average of the area: soups €4-6, some mains €18-20.

Admiralty Lodge
Spanish Point, Miltown Malbay, Co. Clare
T: 065 708 5007 W: www.admiralty.ie
Opening Times: Restaurant closed Mon nights
Directions: *[Map Ref. 18] In Miltown Malbay follow signs for Spanish Point, go past beach for a mile, turn left at T-junction*

One of the latest additions to County Clare's smart line in country houses/boutique hotels. (What is it about this county that it has so many small, chic, dependable, luxurious places to stay?) Admiralty Lodge is right beside Spanish Point Links and caters to golfers. There's a helipad on site, which is a bit Celtic Tiger-ish, but anyone (including non-golfers) would be delighted to stay in this quiet, discreet, marvellously comfortable and impeccably serviced guesthouse, just a short walk from Spanish Point Beach. Bedrooms have four-posters, marble baths, leather sofas and surround sound. Views are less interesting, but that's the only minus. B&B €80-135pps. The Piano Room restaurant has a grand piano that is played on weekend nights, and it serves thoughtful, elegant, classical food. The set dinner is good value at €39.

Munster | Co. Clare

Mount Vernon

Flaggy Shore, New Quay, Co. Clare
T: 065 707 8126 **W:** www.hiddenireland.com/mountvernon
Opening Times: Apr-end Oct
Directions: *[Map Ref. 19]* New Quay, between Kinvara and Ballyvaughan

Be warned: staying here really is like being the guest of a country house. There are only four bedrooms, so there's plenty of interaction with your hosts and other guests, especially at dinnertime. Views are of the garden or the sea, and all are spectacular. A house with a venerable history, it only recently opened to guests. Built in 1788 for Colonel William Persse (a friend of George Washington's) and named after Washington's plantation in Virginia, it subsequently passed into the hands of Sir Hugh Lane, Ireland's greatest art connoisseur. After he drowned in the *Lusitania* in 1915, it became the summer residence of his aunt, Lady Gregory, so Yeats, Synge and Shaw stayed here. It's full of antiques including Augustus John chimney-pieces, has great views of Galway Bay, and is in the Burren. Close to Lahinch and Doonbeg golf courses, but best suited to those who like country walks and Irish culture. B&B €99-110pps, but ask about special deals when you phone. Dinner should be booked in advance.

Mount Vernon, New Quay

Munster | Co. Cork

County Cork

Introduction

The real coastal beauties of Cork are concentrated around the west, starting at Kinsale, rightly famous for its buzzy restaurants and cafes. The Beara Peninsula, among the country's wildest, most romantic spots, has spectacular views of Kenmare and Bantry bays, along with golden beaches, rugged cliffs and windswept moors. At Mizen Head, the southernmost tip of Ireland, is a lighthouse reached by a suspension bridge across a rocky chasm, with sheer cliffs around. Below are the sandy beaches of Barley Cove. Rosscarbery has two Blue Flag beaches, The Warren and Owenahincha, while Skibbereen has the magnificent six-kilometre Tragumna Beach. The natural harbour of Berehaven is a fine spot for fishing, and is usually mobbed with yachts and windsurfers.

By the Water's Edge | Coastal Retreats | 53

Munster | Co. Cork

One of Kinsale's trademark colourful houses

Bayview Hotel

Ballycotton, Co. Cork
T: 021 464 6746 **W:** www.thebayviewhotel.com
Opening Times: Closed Nov-Apr
Directions: *[Map Ref. 1] Turn on to R632 from Castlemartyr (direction Garryvoe); hotel above village*

With its elevated aspect, the Bayview Hotel has spectacular views over the rugged coastline of Ballycotton and its lighthouse. The terraced gardens have paths that run down to the beach, and you may, on occasion, spot a chef picking fresh herbs from the garden. Its restaurant, Capricho, is very well liked, and serves great food with a French slant on Irish meat, fish and fowl. The communal areas are cosy, with dark wood, leather, deep reds and open fires. Touches of modern decor are found in the bedrooms, which are

Munster | Co. Cork

spacious, modern and bright, with good bathrooms (from €85pps, breakfast included). All of the rooms, bar two, enjoy the best seascape that nature can offer. This is a small hotel – only 35 rooms – so there's no pool. Ballycotton is a traditional and unspoiled fishing village. Aspiring sea-anglers and birdwatchers will love this place.

Annie's Restaurant ⓧ €

Main Street, Ballydehob, Co. Cork
T: 028 37292
Opening Times: Dinner only; Tue-Sat
Directions: *[Map Ref. 2] Centre of village on street side*
This West Cork restaurant is personable, quirky and legendary, rather like its proprietor, Annie Barry. The quaint old shopfront simply says 'Annie's'. Inside you'll find an intimate, simply decorated room with just enough elbow space. There's no space to wait around for a table, so head across the road to Levis' pub. Peruse the menu over a G&T and the famous Annie will return to take your order before collecting you when the table is ready. Start with the mussels (€10), follow with the catch of the day (€29.90), and finish with some great Gubbeen. Book well in advance.

Casey's of Baltimore

Baltimore, Co. Cork
T: 028 20197 **W:** www.caseysofbaltimore.com
Opening Times: Year round
Directions: *[Map Ref. 3] On right as you enter village from Skibbereen direction*
This hotel is a local institution. Located just outside Baltimore, it enjoys amazing views over Roaring Water Bay. Beware, though: some rooms are in need of a bit of jazzing up. On the up side, most have amazing sea views and are very spacious (Room 30 has the best view; €75pps, breakfast included). The bar has live music on Saturday nights and can be noisy, so if you want restful sleep rather than a rousing pub session, look elsewhere. The bar food is decent, and breakfast offers some lovely home-made soda bread and scones, as well as the requisite full Irish. The restaurant has great views, friendly service and some excellent seafood. There's also an outdoor seating area, for when the weather permits. It's a bit 'Oirish' - fiddles and traditional Irish pub decor abound - but a great spot to immerse yourself in the local hospitality.

By the Water's Edge | Coastal Retreats

Munster | Co. Cork

The Mews ⓧ
Baltimore, Co. Cork
T: 028 20910 **W:** www.mewsrestaurant.com
Opening Times: May-Oct; closed Sun
Directions: *[Map Ref. 4] Centre of village; signposted before harbour*

Pull your chair in close and settle in for a romantic evening in this bijou restaurant and art gallery – stone walls, white linen, soft candlelight, and no hurry to leave. There are unlikely to be two sittings or a rush to go anywhere else. Try the carpaccio of beef with horseradish sauce and hazelnut cream (€12.95) or some chowder. For a main, you could do worse than a rack of lamb (€28.95), but given its location on the lip of the Atlantic, you should really opt for the catch of the day (€26.95). The Mews pulls in an arty, bohemian, and typically West Cork crowd.

Ballylickey House
Ballylickey, Bantry Bay, Co. Cork
T: 027 50071 **W:** www.ballylickeymanorhouse.com
Opening Times: Mar-Nov
Directions: *[Map Ref. 5] Between Bantry and Glengariff on N71*

Originally built as a shooting lodge by Lord Kenmare, Ballylickey House has been in the Graves family for over four generations. As the name suggests, there is an artistic connection to the poet Robert Graves, an uncle of the current owners. This secluded manor has stunning views over Bantry Bay (€60pps, breakfast included) and rests upon beautiful grounds. B&B is offered in the main house and in the sprinkling of pretty cottages clustered around the heated outdoor swimming pool. Lots of Laura Ashley-type soft furnishings throughout, which shouldn't work together, but do, adding to the cultured ambience of the place. Looking for a spot of fishing, walking, canoodling? Look no further.

Blairs Cove House ⓧ
Durrus, Bantry, Co. Cork
T: 027 61127 **W:** www.blairscove.ie
Opening Times: Year round
Directions: *[Map Ref. 6] From Durrus take R591 to Goleen/Barleycove; 2 kilometres outside village, through blue gate on right-hand side*

Munster | Co. Cork

Blairs Cove sits on four and a half acres of blooming gardens and land, overlooking Dunmanus Bay. The house dates back to 1760, and its stables and outhouses have been converted into four apartments and two cottages that offer B&B or self-catering accommodation. All apartments have en suite bathrooms, mezzanines and huge windows with breathtaking views of the water or the mountains to the rear. (The apartment over the restaurant, Blairs Cove 4, offers the best sea view; €110pps in peak season, breakfast included.) While Sabine and Philippe de Mey run the accommodation, the restaurant is leased out separately, but is similarly impressive. The interior resembles a converted church, with exposed walls and high beams. Get ready to be dazzled by the crystal chandelier, as well as the buffet of starters. Meats are cooked on an open fire, and desserts served on a grand piano. Outdoor seating is also available, so you can enjoy the lily pond and immaculate courtyard on a long summer evening.

O'Connor's Seafood Restaurant ❌ €

The Square, Bantry, Co. Cork
T: 027 50221 W: www.oconnorseafood.com
Opening Times: Closed bank holidays, Sun (May-Oct)
Directions: *[Map Ref. 7] Main square, town centre*
The model sailboats in the window immediately catch the eye and

O'Connor's Seafood Restaurant, Bantry

Munster | Co. Cork

offer a hit-over-the-head clue to the theme of this restaurant. Don't be mislead, however – this is no dusty old wreck with shabby nautical memorabilia and worse-for-wear fishermen in a dark corner. Instead you'll find a modern restaurant with gentile ship-chic touches. Think exposed white-painted brickwork, candelabra and chandeliers. Try to book the booth tables 6 and 9, which feel like you're onboard an old elegant ocean-liner. Decor aside, the seafood is tremendous. Try the oysters grilled with lemon (€7 for three) and the Bantry Bay mussels in Murphy's Irish stout, (€10.50). Booking advised.

Seaview House Hotel

Ballylickey, Bantry, Co. Cork
T: 027 50462 W: www.seaviewhousehotel.com
Opening Times: Mid-Mar to mid-Nov
Directions: *[Map Ref. 8] From Bantry take N71 to Glengariff; 10-minute drive*
The name of this country house hotel is a little misleading. There are distant views of Bantry Bay, but it's difficult to see through the trees, so don't come here hoping to have an uninterrupted view of the water. However, bedrooms are generally large, with appealing mahogany beds and spacious modern bathrooms (suites with

Seaview House Hotel, Bantry

Munster | Co. Cork

balconies from €80pps, breakfast included). Gardens are very impressive, as is the welcome and the house, which is filled with period furniture and interesting antiques. There are plenty of communal places to relax: a library, a small bar and a pleasant living room with an open fire. This house is more suitable to couples and older people looking for relaxation. The conservatory restaurant, which feels more like a breakfast room, offers a five-course table d'hôte menu.

The Snug €
The Quay, Bantry, Co. Cork
T: 027 50057
Opening Times: Food served until 9pm
Directions: *[Map Ref. 9] The Quay, beside Garda station*
Typical pub grub, so opt for the daily roast or a cracking home-made soup and a tasty open sandwich. This busy pub, on Bantry's Quay, attracts a loyal local clientele, as well as plenty of tourists who invade the West Cork town every summer. Settle down for a bite in the cosy wood-dominated interior. This pub has an easygoing philosophy and it fills up quickly, particularly at the weekend. The kind of place that fills up rapidly, so you may be waiting a while for your pint, but it's well worth it - hearty food, lots of quality local produce, and the Guinness is sublime.

Deasy's Harbour Bar and Restaurant ✕ €
Ring Village Clonakilty, Co. Cork
T: 023 35741
Opening Times: Closed Mon-Tue; dinner Wed-Sat, lunch Sun
Directions: *[Map Ref. 10] Village centre, opposite water*
Like an old shipwreck, this is a great discovery. The waterside location, in the village of Ring, overlooking Clonakilty Bay, is enough to bring you there, but the food at Deasy's will make your journey extra-worthwhile. The emphasis is on seafood – scallops, monkfish and hake (the most expensive fish dish is €28.95) – but they do a great steak also. Its wooden-beamed interior is atmospheric, cosy and candlelit, conjuring up images of old seafaring days. The view through the huge windows is beautiful, come rain or shine, but a break in the clouds serves the outside seating area best. Service may be slow when busy, but you'll always get a smile. Parking is a problem, though, with only four spaces available at the front. Good-value Sunday lunch (three courses €32).

By the Water's Edge | Coastal Retreats

Munster | Co. Cork

Inchydoney Island Lodge and Spa, Clonakilty

Inchydoney Island Lodge and Spa
Clonakilty, Co. Cork
T: 023 33143 W: www.inchydoneyisland.com
Opening Times: Year round
Directions: *[Map Ref. 11] From Cork, N71 to Clonakilty, then causeway to Inchydoney*

The real star of this retreat just might be Inchydoney Beach, which is truly spectacular. However, although the hotel is severely modern on approach, once inside, with a complimentary orange juice or Irish Mist in hand, you will find yourself very happy. The lobby is roomy and inviting, with plenty of sofas, chairs and open fires for lounging around while sipping a post-dinner brandy. Spa treatments are great (facials €80-130), however, on a recent visit, the pool area needed some TLC. The majority of rooms now have balconies (Inchydoney suites, weekend and peak-season B&B

Munster | Co. Cork

€300pps), which make them feel bigger, but the trendy decor in some of the rooms is strangely dark for a seaside location, and some of the patterns are overpowering. The espresso machine is a nice touch. Food is served in the bar, noon-9pm, and dinner is served in the Gulfstream Restaurant (€65 set menu available), which has panoramic views of the beach. Service is invariably friendly and helpful, but the hotel can get very busy at weekends, when families flock to the area to use the ample facilities. This is a real getaway. Take an early morning walk along the seashore and reconnect with nature.

Richy's Bar and Bistro

Wolfetone Street, Clonakilty, Co. Cork
T: 023 21852 W: www.richysbarandbistro.com
Opening Times: Year round
Directions: *[Map Ref. 12] Follow N71 from Cork to Clonakilty, take third exit off roundabout; 300 yards on right*

A Mauritian chef plying his trade in the 'meat and potato' territory that is West Cork? Scallops and black pudding? There are lots of reasons why Richy's Bar and Bistro shouldn't work, but nobody told ebullient chef-owner Richy Virahsawmy. You could go into five different bars in Clonakilty on a Friday, asking about a decent spot for dinner the next night, and hear Richy's mentioned by everyone. It's a local triumph, with food that combines fusion cooking with some of the best ingredients in the country. Specials are chalked up on a blackboard every day, but if you're merely passing through, make sure at least one of you tries Richy's Mauritian-style curry – not exactly Corkonian, but enough to take your mind off the rain bucketing down outside for an hour or so.

Shanley's

Connolly Street, Clonakilty, Co. Cork
T: 023 33790
Opening Times: Year round
Directions: *[Map Ref. 13] Follow N71 from Cork to Clonakilty*

It may attract a slightly older crowd, but regulars to Shanley's pub know that this locals' local is one of the best nightspots in West Cork. As well as boasting one of the best pints of Guinness around and an inviting snug, Shanley's is a hotspot for Irish music – just check out the crowds that descend on the venue during Cork Jazz Week. When Jimi Hendrix's bass player, Noel Redding, moved to

Munster | Co. Cork

Richy Virahsawmy, of Richy's Bar and Bistro, Clonakilty

Clonakilty in the early '70s to escape the excesses of the American music scene, rather than maintain a low profile, the erstwhile bassist set himself up with a gig or two in Shanley's, thus impressing himself firmly on the community. And he's not the only one ... be warned – after a couple of pints of the black stuff, you might end up on stage yourself.

Knockeven House

Rushbrooke, Cobh, Co. Cork
T: 021 481 1778 W: www.knockevenhouse.com
Opening Times: Year round
Directions: *[Map Ref. 14] Outskirts of Cobh; signposted*
This house dates back to the 1840s, and has the posture of an elegant aunt who loves her Waterford crystal. The interior is pretty luxurious for a B&B, all heavy drapes and floral fabric, with an open fire in the welcoming drawing room. The bedrooms are large with mini-chandeliers and dark-wood antique touches (from €50pps, breakfast included). They also have modern en suites with power showers. Front bedrooms have lovely views over gardens, and birds are more likely to rouse you from slumber than cars. Nothing is left to chance by Pam, the proprietor and hostess, who serves tea and scones on her best china. Breakfast is great, with options of fresh fruit salad and cheese, as well as cooked options. A fluffy-robe kind of place.

Munster | Co. Cork

Sheraton Hotel and Spa 🌍 ♿

Fota Island, Cobh, Co. Cork
T: 021 467 3000 W: www.fotaisland.ie
Opening Times: Year round; restaurant Tue-Sat
Directions: *[Map Ref. 15] From Cork take N25 east for 5 kilometres, take left, follow signs*

An unusually relaxed and friendly five-star resort on Fota Island, with views of the famous golf course and parkland, this hotel's cumbersome and rather ugly facade caused consternation when first built. However, time and a bit of planting healed the rift, and this is a good hotel. The lobby is medieval-like in decor: velvet upholstery, candelabra, stone slabs and wooden beams. However, beyond the lobby you'll find a wholly modern experience. Rooms are large, with king-size beds, and the colour schemes unfussy – think neutral hues and splashes of colour. Bathrooms are huge, with wetrooms and baths made to share (peak-season deluxe suite €167pps, breakfast included). The five-star prices really hit home, though, when you need to eat. A sandwich in the bar will set you back €15.50, and the full Irish (if not included in your deal) costs €22. There are also two restaurants: The Cove, which is fine dining, and the Fota Restaurant, which is bistro-style; both are good but expensive. The spa area is worth exploring, but use of the hydrotherapy pool will cost an extra €25.

Cronin's Pub €

Point Road, Crosshaven, Co. Cork
T: 021 483 1829 W: www.croninspub.com
Opening Times: Closed Jan; restaurant closed Sun-Mon
Directions: *[Map Ref. 16] Village centre, beside car park*

There is a wealth of local history at this traditional waterfront pub. Enjoy a pint and an education as you examine the black-and-white photographs and myriad of artefacts on display. Cronin's is a hugely popular local pub and a first-stop destination for holidaying Corkonians and thirsty sailors. The outside seating area by the harbour gets a little crazy in summer, and the bar food goes down a storm. The Mad Fish seafood restaurant at Cronin's is run by the surf-mad Denis Cronin and is doing a brisk trade, but only seats 35, so there is much competition for tables. It's the mussels (€15) that's the main draw here - succulent, piled high, and straight off the boat. The salt-and-pepper squid is also a joy at just €8. There's also some meat (steak €23) and a random Thai curry (€15) thrown in. A very West Cork enterprise, but an unpretentious and atmospheric one.

By the Water's Edge | Coastal Retreats

Munster | Co. Cork

The Heron's Cove

The Harbour, Goleen, West Cork
T: 028 35225 W: www.heronscove.com
Opening Times: Year round
Directions: *[Map Ref. 17] Left in Goleen Village to harbour; 300 metres*

Not a party-people destination. This restaurant with rooms overlooks Goleen Harbour, a remote part of West Cork. There's not a lot to do, but that's the point. Watch the tide ebb and flow in the harbour, spot the birds hovering over the water, take a coastal walk, or visit nearby Mizen Head. The house is like a large family home, and the rooms are basic but clean. Three out of five have balconies and sea views (€45pps). Dinner at the Heron's Cove should involve crab cakes and Bantry Bay mussels. Unusually, you

Casino House, Kilbrittain, Co. Cork

Munster | Co. Cork

choose your wine from a rack rather than a menu. Service is good, but when busy, can show cracks. The restaurant has a casual, country interior with varnished wood, delph on the wall and a grandfather clock gently ticking away.

Casino House ⓧ

Coolmain Bay, Kilbrittain, Co. Cork
T: 023 49944
Opening Hours: Closed Jan-Feb
Directions: *[Map Ref. 18] On R600 between Kinsale and Timoleague*
The furthest inland of all our entries (a few miles west of Kinsale), Casino House is well worth the detour, particularly for the food. Kerrin and Michael Relja run a charming old house that has minimalist decor (think old-world Irish cottage with Scandinavian detail – the owners' attention to interior design is obvious). The locally sourced cuisine is excellent, too, but be warned: the restaurant is very small (and slightly chilly in winter), with 35 covers including outdoor dining. Superb home-made breads are not worth missing, particularly when accompanied by the Ummera organic smoked salmon. The wine list is also well selected to complement the food. The Casino Cottage sleeps two (€85 per night/€155 two nights, not including breakfast, which shouldn't be missed.)

Glen Country House

Kilbrittain, Co. Cork
T: 023 49862 **W:** www.glencountryhouse.com
Opening Times: Easter-Nov
Directions: *[Map Ref. 19] Midway between Kinsale and Clonakilty; signposted off R600*
Home from home, albeit it a very stylish one. From the home-made scones and jam that greet you after a long car journey, to the fact that you can bring your pet – it's all so soothing. This elegant farmhouse, draped in ivy, has views over Courtmacsherry Bay and the Atlantic Ocean. The four large bedrooms are en suite. Floral-fabric touches in the rooms, but not fussy (request Room 4 for the best sea view; B&B €60pps). Soft linen on comfortable beds ensures a wonderful sleep. There is an emphasis on all things organic – eggs from family hens, vegetables from the walled garden, bacon from free-range pigs. The old photographs on the wall give an intimate feel, and the colourful wildflowers in the breakfast room add a natural prettiness to proceedings.

By the Water's Edge | COASTAL RETREATS

Munster | Co. Cork

Blue Haven Hotel
3-4 Pearse Street, Kinsale, Co. Cork
T: 021 477 2209 W: www.bluehavenkinsale.com
Opening Times: Year round
Directions: *[Map Ref. 20] Town centre*

This boutique hotel, in the heart of Kinsale, sits on the site of the old fish market. The hotel's Restaurant Blu, with its glitzy decor, is popular with locals who choose from a menu of seafood, steak and a couple of poultry dishes. The addition of a cocktail bar has added more weight to its glamorous boutique ambition. Rooms are slightly cramped with too much furniture, but are comfortable, with modern and neutral tones (deluxe room, peak season €80-97pps, breakfast included). The Molton Brown toiletries are a nice touch. No parking on the hotel grounds, but there is free parking nearby. Staff are super-helpful, and although some parts of the hotel are by now a little jaded, they are being gradually modernised.

Blue Haven Hotel, Kinsale

Fishy Fishy Café
Crowley's Quay, Kinsale, Co. Cork
T: 021 470 0415 W: www.fishyfishy.ie
Opening Times: Year round
Directions: *[Map Ref. 21] On Kinsale Harbour*

There are now two reasons to queue in Kinsale. A bigger, brighter and better-located Fishy Fishy Café opened in 2006 on the harbourfront, to a chorus of approval. Brighter and roomier than its elder sibling, it is also stylish and Aqua Mint fresh, with clean-cut wood and splashes of seaside blue. They have retained the original Fishy Fishy Café, which also houses a deli counter. The new

Munster | Co. Cork

restaurant continues the infamous Fishy Fishy policies of no reservations, limited opening hours (noon-4.30pm) and cash only. But none of that is a deterrent. There are stunning views across the harbour and seating outside under massive parasols. The food is wholesome and delicious, with the catch cooked simply and shown utter respect. This is a proper dining experience.

Harbour Lodge
Scilly, Kinsale, Co. Cork
T: 021 477 2376 W: www.harbourlodge.com
Opening Times: Year round
Directions: *[Map Ref. 22] Scilly waterfront, beside Spinnaker pub*
A waterfront B&B located at the edge of Kinsale Harbour. Some unusual touches of luxury: you'll find a robe, slippers and port in your room, as well as a turndown service. The offer of a glass of champagne upon arrival is also very seductive. The rooms are large and contemporary, with bright, uncluttered decor, helped along by big brass beds and generously sized en suites. Top-floor rooms all have their own balconies and overlook the harbour (B&B from €99pps). Breakfast is served in the conservatory, which has beautiful views of Kinsale, as is dinner (three-course set menu €38). On the downside, service can be a little grumpy. It's not especially glam and is slightly overpriced, but the setting is romantic and the location very peaceful. The Spinnaker pub next door serves pub grub and is handy for a couple of nightcaps.

Jim Edwards €
Market Quay, Kinsale, Co. Cork
T: 021 477 2541 W: www.jimedwardskinsale.com
Opening Times: Year round
Directions: *[Map Ref. 23] Town centre*
You won't find anything too fancy-pants here. This is a convivial, character-filled town-centre pub and restaurant, with a comfortable varnished wood interior. Fake oil lamps and real candles help to light the restaurant in the evening, which is an atmospheric plus. Choose your lobsters from the tank and enjoy them with a hearty beurre sauce. Steaks are a good bet also. Bar food on offer is samey – think chicken wings and scampi, washed down with a decent pint of the black stuff. This being Kinsale, the pub can get very busy. Not a bad thing, but you may need to flail your arms a little to get some service.

Munster | Co. Cork

Old Bank House, Kinsale

Man Friday
Scilly, Kinsale, Co. Cork
T: 021 477 2260 **W:** www.manfridaykinsale.ie
Opening Times: Closed Sun
Directions: *[Map Ref. 24]* Above harbour at Scilly

Man Friday sits high above Kinsale Harbour and looks down on a pretty congregation of boats bobbing up and down on the water and town lights twinkling. The restaurant is set over four levels and has a garden terrace. The old-school, dark wood interior hasn't changed much over the years and could do with a bit of TLC, but locals and visitors alike keep coming back for the view and the food. Seafood plays a big part, with monkfish (€28.95) and the crab au gratin (€11.50) house specialties. They're not ashamed to keep old favourites on the menu: Marie Rose hasn't returned as a retro nod – it actually never left.

Old Bank House
11 Pearse Street, Kinsale, Co. Cork
T: 021 477 4075 W: www.oldbankhousekinsale.com
Opening Times: Year round
Directions: *[Map Ref. 25] Village centre, beside post office*
This Georgian townhouse is an upmarket sister to the Blue Haven Hotel, with an equally central location in Kinsale. It is marketed as the classiest B&B in town, and to be fair, for the most part, it is - during our last visit, the lobby and common areas were undergoing a welcome refurb. Rooms are prettily decorated with large beds, antiques, off-white colour schemes and high-glamour soft furnishings, as well as the odd chandelier. Bathrooms are modern and a good size, with mirrors big enough not to fight over. The pillow menu is a nice touch – choose from feather or foam. The Collection Suite is particularly desirable (€125-130pps, peak season, breakfast included), with a private sitting room and jacuzzi. The arrival of Café Number 11 has added a nice option for lunch on the premises.

The Spaniard Inn
Scilly, Kinsale, Co. Cork
T: 021 477 243 W: www.thespaniard.ie
Opening Times: Year round; restaurant closed two weeks (Nov, Jan)
Directions: *[Map Ref. 26] Half a kilometre south-east of Kinsale*
Like the jolly Cornish sailors who settled in Scilly, you too may be drawn to the Spaniard Inn by the music, the welcome and the ale. Named after Don Juan d'Aquila, a courageous Spanish soldier who took part in the Battle of Kinsale, this place has plenty of atmosphere, created by people with salt in their veins. The views over Kinsale are amazing, and the bar serves well-received dishes with a typical seafaring vibe. Try the oysters in Guinness (€5 for three) or the famous Spaniard Inn chowder (€7.50). The restaurant is seasonal and an eager crowd-pleaser, with an extensive menu of fish (sea bass with caper and lemon butter €20.50) or Irish rib-eye (€24). The restaurant is split-level, with wooden beams almost tipping your head and sturdy wooden furniture. Slam your tankard of ale on the table in time with the music – it's that type of place.

Munster | Co. Cork

The Spaniard, Kinsale

O'Callaghan Walshe

North Square, Rosscarbery, Co. Cork
T: 023 48125 **W:** www.ocallaghanwalshe.com
Opening Times: Closed Mon; weekends only off-season
Directions: *[Map Ref. 27] Main square, Rosscarbery*

The old bar frontage may lead you to believe that this place only serves the black stuff. Don't be fooled. Seafood is the main player, with a few other token dishes thrown in for sworn carnivores. This restaurant, on the main square in Rosscarbery, is a favourite seafood destination for locals and tourists, who quickly appreciate its staunch reputation for fine food and conviviality. Owner Sean Kearney is always on hand to recommend a dish, and he's usually right. Fish comes straight from the boats, and oysters, scallops, turbot and sea bass – day-fresh – are all cooked to perfection (starters €8.50-21.50; mains €29.50-50, for a whole Rosscarbery lobster). The quirky dining room is perfectly accessorised by fishing

Munster | Co. Cork

nets, sturdy used furniture, and a collection of old wine bottles. Dine by candlelight for increased ambience. Finish with the sticky toffee pudding. Pricey, but worth it.

Grove House
Colla Road, Schull, Co. Cork
T: 028 28067 W: www.grovehouseschull.com
Opening Times: Restaurant open weekends only off-season
Directions: *[Map Ref. 28] Just outside village, beside Church of Ireland*

This quirky Georgian guesthouse and restaurant overlooks Schull Harbour and has a distinct Scandinavian slant. Where else would you find three types of home-pickled herring (€8) on the menu in West Cork? If that doesn't tickle your fancy, then there are plenty of more familiar meat and fish dishes on offer. Katarina Runske and her son, Nico, run this laid-back house. Ignore the occasionally untidy appearance – Grove House has charm and is a homey spot. The house was extensively renovated ten years ago, which means you'll find pine floors and some contemporary touches amid restored original features. Bedrooms are big, with comfy old iron beds and large en suite bathrooms. Three rooms out of five have a view of the water (€50pps, breakfast included). There's also a lovely outside terrace to kick back with a glass of wine and watch the boats go by.

Stanley House
Schull, Co. Cork
T: 028 28425 W: www.stanley-house.net
Opening Times: End Mar-Oct
Directions: *[Map Ref. 29] Top of Main Street; signposted*

As simple B&Bs go, this place is almost faultless. The house is immaculate, with hanging baskets and enough whitewash to blind you. Then there's the view over the fields and down to the sea. Bedrooms (€38pps) are on the small side, but have everything you need: tea- and coffee-making facilities and a hairdryer. Then there is the lady at the helm, Nancy Brosnan, whose welcome is as legendary as her breakfasts: full Irish, kippers, or smoked salmon and scrambled eggs. Tap into her local knowledge to enrich your visit to Schull. If you are lucky enough, you'll even grab sight of Nancy's herd of deer as they gather near the house. This is total relaxation with a surrogate mother.

Munster | Co. Cork

T.J. Newman's/Newman's West €
Main Street, Schull, Co. Cork
T: 028 27776 **W:** www.tjnewmans.com
Opening Times: Year round
Directions: *[Map Ref. 30] Main Street, Schull*
This is a clever operation. The Corner House, with its old-man pub-front and snug interior, has remained unchanged for 100 years, and still attracts people over land and water for a welcome pint. However, Newman's West, the cafe/wine bar that has replaced the old off-licence next door, has hit the ground running, and is a roaring success. The interior may seem a little too cafe-like for night-time dining, with its lemon walls and modern furniture, but don't let that turn you off. The menu is vast and serves great food all day, from breakfast pancakes with bacon (€4.90) to a lunchtime sandwich (Club West BLT €4.90) or a warming dinner of fish pie (€8.90). It even has a lengthy cocktail menu. Piña Colada, anyone? Respect to the old and a nod to the new.

Mary Ann's Bar and Restaurant ✗ ♿ €
Castletownshend, Skibbereen, Co. Cork
T: 028 36146 **W:** www.westcorkweek.com/maryanns
Opening Times: Closed three weeks in Jan and Mon in winter
Directions: *[Map Ref. 31] 5 miles from Skibbereen; 52 miles from Cork*
This historic pub and restaurant, dating back to 1846, has been lovingly maintained, and little changed. The attractive painted facade befits this old-world pub, which serves killer seafood platters in summer (€32.95, serves two). There is an extensive bar-food menu that concentrates on local seafood (catch of the day €14.95) and is easily restaurant standard. The fine-dining restaurant upstairs also specialises in seafood, but offers some good options for meat-eaters, too. An outside seating area is available for dining al fresco and has an all-weather retractable canopy. This is a well-run enterprise. No surprise, then, that it is dripping with awards and recommendations. Try the brown bread and enjoy its hands-on hospitality. The maître d' is larger than life and will make you feel instantly at home.

Munster | Co. Kerry

County Kerry

Introduction

Kerry has perhaps the most impressive coastline on the island, making up about 12 per cent of the total shoreline. Dominated by peninsulas and inlets carved out by the Atlantic Ocean over hundreds of millennia, Kerry has the Dingle, Beara and Iveragh peninsulas, each with its own natural wonders and idyllic towns and villages. The Iveragh Peninsula – the largest of the three – is also home to the Macgillicuddy Reeks, a mountain range that boasts Ireland's tallest mountain, Carrauntohill. It's a coast that has claimed many victims over the years, including the galleons of the Spanish Armada and German U-boats, but is by far one of the most inherently beautiful parts of the country. The rugged shoreline is echoed by the many islands that pepper the surrounding ocean, including the Blaskets, Valentia Island and the magical Skelligs, the larger of which has a medieval monastery clinging to the top of a bare rocky outcrop.

By the Water's Edge | Coastal Retreats | 73

Munster | Co. Kerry

Munster | Co. Kerry

Íragh Tí Connor
Main Street, Ballybunion, Co. Kerry
T: 068 27112 W: www.golfballybunion.com
Opening Times: Closed Dec-Jan
Directions: *[Map Ref. 1] Ballybunion Main Street, opposite statue of Bill Clinton*

John and Joan O'Connor run a great guesthouse – the name means 'inheritance of O'Connor' – on the edge of the golfing town of Ballybunion. It's really more of a small hotel – there's a bar, a restaurant and they can cater for conferences. No sea view, but a lovely walled garden and a conservatory, where they serve afternoon tea. The rooms are generously sized, especially the suites, and have antiques and marble bathtubs. A lot of quiet luxury here. B&B from €80pps. Trivia: the life-size bronze statue of Bill Clinton swinging his golf club across the road is the only statue of Clinton in the world (although the Kosovans are planning a 10-foot homage in Pristina).

Derrynane Hotel and Restaurant
Caherdaniel, Co. Kerry
T: 066 947 5136 W: www.derrynane.com
Opening Times: Easter-Oct
Directions: *[Map Ref. 2] Ring of Kerry*

Location and service is what makes Mary O'Connor's hotel stand out. The building is 1960s chic – long, low, discreet, rather than big and showy – and constructed so that most rooms face Kenmare Bay. Caherdaniel is a top location, with one of the most beautiful beaches in Ireland. Golf close by, and plenty of history in the Daniel O'Connell House. The hotel also has a stunning outdoor pool and a spa with seaweed therapy. Its glass-fronted restaurant faces the sea. With those views, anything would taste good, but the food doesn't rest on its laurels. Set menu €39. B&B from €49pps. For more luxury accommodation, check out the holiday homes on site – brand-new and very chic, and have the use of the hotel facilities. They sleep six adults. (€550 per week, winter months; up to €1,600 per week, high season).

Opposite: Inch Strand, Co. Kerry

Munster | Co. KERRY

Derrynane House, Caherdaniel

Derrynane House Tea Rooms €
Caherdaniel, Co. Kerry
T: 066 947 5113
Opening Times: 1pm-6pm, Apr-Oct
Directions: *[Map Ref. 3] 3.5 kilometres from Caherdaniel Village*
The first reason to come to Derrynane House, ancestral home of Daniel O'Connell, is to see the enormous gold and purple chariot that took him from gaol home to Merrion Square in 1844. The second is to eat in the tea rooms (right beside the chariot house). Delicious toasties with cheese, freshly cut onion and proper, thick ham; lovely quiches and robust salads, but it's the cakes that really hit home. Walk across the dunes after a swim for your afternoon tea here.

Iskeroon
Caherdaniel, Co. Kerry
T: 066 947 5119 W: www.iskeroon.com
Opening Times: May-Sep
Directions: *[Map Ref. 4] On road from Waterville to Caherdaniel, turn off at Scariff Inn, drive down hill towards Bunavalla Pier, turn left at pier, through gate*

Munster | Co. Kerry

There's a minimum two-night stay. This isn't a quick stop on the way to somewhere – it's an end destination. If you do succeed in getting a booking, you'll want to stay longer. Geraldine Burkitt and David Hare's wonderfully situated and beautifully renovated home is lauded by everyone from Condé Nast to the *Washington Post*. And they only charge €80pps. Down a steep and winding road off the Ring of Kerry, Iskeroon has four and a half acres of tropical gardens and overlooks Derrynane Harbour. It's on the more isolated, secluded part of the strand, and the house has its own pier. Just two suites and a self-catering apartment, all located in the renovated and very stylish coach house, and all with sea views. There are never more than six guests at a time, so get booking!

Spillane's
Maharees, Castlegregory, Co. Kerry
T: 066 713 9125 W: www.spillanesbar.com
Opening Times: Closed Nov-Mar
Directions: *[Map Ref. 5] From Castlegregory, follow signs for Fahamore (4 miles)*

It's big, it's busy, it's on the longest beach in Ireland. If you haven't booked, expect to wait. This place opened in 1875 as a general-goods store, and Michael and Marilyn Spillane are the fifth generation of the family looking after the public. Food is pub grub at its best, with the emphasis on seafood and steaks. The specials change daily, but expect monkfish, crab claws, and mussels. Kids will like the burgers and pasta.

Ashe's Seafood Bar and B&B
Main Street, Dingle, Co. Kerry
T: 066 915 0989 W: www.ashesseafoodbar.com
Opening Times: Closed Sun
Directions: *[Map Ref. 6] Main Street, Dingle Town*

Restaurateurs in Dingle are vying for your custom. Nobody gets away with standard touristic fare for long. Ashe's is among the best in a competitive market. This is an intelligent, well-thought-out restaurant with solid, traditional seafood, locally sourced steaks and lamb, and a short but strong wine list. Decor is cosy and old-school. Try the Spanish fish stew, somewhat pricey (€28.95), but the real thing. They now also offer rooms upstairs – clean and functional. No breakfast, but good value at €25pps.

Munster | Co. KERRY

Ballintaggart House, Dingle

Ballintaggart House
Ballintaggart, Dingle, Co. Kerry
T: 066 915 1333 W: www.ballintaggarthouse.com
Opening Times: Year round; restaurant Tue-Sun
Directions: *[Map Ref. 7] On Dingle/Tralee road, just before Dingle Town*

The exterior of this 300-year-old manor is unadorned grey stone, but the highly polished windows give it away: within is comfort, understated luxury and perfectly chosen furnishings. Until last year a much-loved hostel, it survived intact all those backpackers, and is now a luxury guesthouse with six spacious en suite bedrooms (B&B €65-85pps). The baths have claws, there are Victorian screens to change behind, and each room has its own character. Panoramic views give onto mountains and sea. Owner John Cluskey used to

Munster | Co. Kerry

own the award-winning restaurant Doyle's of Dingle, so food is a feature here: porridge and eggs from local hens at breakfast, and fish stew or oysters for dinner (served Tue-Sun, approximately €50pps). Just a few minutes' drive from Dingle Town, but completely peaceful. Book it if you can!

Castlewood House

Dingle, Co. Kerry
T: 066 915 2788 W: www.castlewooddingle.com
Opening Times: Closed Jan, Valentine's Day and some of Dec
Directions: *[Map Ref. 8] Take Milltown road from Dingle, half km from town centre, overlooking Dingle Bay*

Staying here is like being in one of those 1980s American soaps – *Dallas*, *Dynasty* or *The Colbys* – everything is big, jazzy, luxurious and mod-con. The baths have jacuzzi settings, the towel rails are heated, the bathrobes are fluffy, the entrance hall is red-carpeted, and the house is built on a rise to take advantage of the views across Dingle Bay. The majority of rooms have views of the bay – ask for the junior or deluxe suites. On a wet Kerry day, or after a five-mile hike, you will be very glad of all this American-style comfort. Castlewood House is new, purpose-built, and run by Brian and Helen Heaton. Brian's parents, Nuala and Cameron, run the long-established Heaton's House next door (another good address), and Brian learned his standards of hospitality from them. The breakfasts go all out: organic smoked salmon, porridge with Baileys, and (our favourite) scrambled eggs with bacon and roasted tomatoes. B&B €50-97.50pps.

The Chart House

The Mall, Dingle, Co. Kerry
T: 066 915 2255
Opening Times: Dinner only; open daily Jun-Sep; restricted winter opening hours (phone to check)
Directions: *[Map Ref. 9] Left as you enter town*

The stone front is on the road, the back looks out over Dingle Harbour, the dining room is rust-red and nautical, and the food is subtle and consistently delicious. Try the Annascaul black pudding for starters (smoother than the more ubiquitous Clonakilty version), then the curried monkfish tails or the Kerry mountain lamb. Expect to pay West Coast average, e.g. starters about €9, mains €24. Finish up with cheese and vintage port.

Munster | Co. Kerry

Dingle Skellig Hotel
Dingle, Co. Kerry
T: 066 915 0200 W: www.dingleskellig.com
Opening Times: Nov to mid-Feb, weekends only
Directions: *[Map Ref. 10] From Tralee/Killarney, on sea side of road just before Dingle*

Owners The Garvey Group also own the Dingle Benner's Hotel, in the centre of town. If you're young, or you like being centrally located, or you like things hip, go to Benner's. The Dingle Skellig has a '70s vibe (we like it, but some complain it's outdated) and a kids' club, so is a family favourite. It also has a superb location on Dingle Bay, but there are 111 rooms of differing quality, so book carefully. The superior rooms/suites on the third floor have the best views. Standard rooms can be as low as €60pps, but you might be on a ground floor without a view. You'll be happy in one of the two presidential suites, but you might be paying €175pps. Great swimming pool, though, a gorgeous outdoor hot tub, and good family deals.

Gorman's Clifftop House and Restaurant
Glaise Bheag, Ballydavid, Dingle Peninsula, Co. Kerry
T: 066 915 5162 W: www.gormans-clifftophouse.com
Opening Times: Year round; restaurant closed Sun
Directions: *[Map Ref. 11] 8 miles west of Dingle Town; signposted 'An Fheothanach'*

This is on the Dingle Way walking route, with Smerwick Harbour in the front and the Brandon Mountains behind. There are spectacular views from the lounge, restaurant, and four of the nine rooms (ask for a junior suite). They also hire bikes. Our advice: stay a few days, walk, bike, swim, and eat in the restaurant, also open to non-residents. B&B €45-75pps. Vincent Gorman produces fresh, healthy food: carrot and courgette soup, Dingle Bay prawns or, for the vegetarians, grilled aubergine and roasted red pepper pie, and this year he's bringing back his popular Irish stew (€14.95). Mains €13.95-28.50.

John Benny Moriarty
Strand Street, Dingle, Co. Kerry
T: 066 915 1215 W: www.johnbennyspub.com
Opening Times: Year round
Directions: *[Map Ref. 12] Opposite pier, Dingle Town*

Munster | Co. Kerry

Gallarus Oratory, Dingle

People come to Dingle for the music, and John Benny Moriarty and his wife, Eilís Kennedy, are well-known trad musicians. Catch a Wednesday night session here. You can get Guinness and Murphy's on draught and eat chowder (€6.95), beef and Guinness stew (€12.95), or battered fish of the day (€13.95). Food served all day. John Benny Moriarty was named one of *Hospitality Ireland* magazine's top three pubs in Ireland.

Milltown House
Dingle, Co. Kerry
T: 066 915 1372 W: www.milltownhousedingle.com
Opening Times: May-Oct
Directions: *[Map Ref. 13] R559 from Dingle Town (Ventry direction), 2 kilometres from town centre*
Set on the shores of Dingle Bay, Milltown House has a great location, which owners Mark and Anne Kerry use to best advantage. Breakfast, from cold meats to stewed apples, is served in the

By the Water's Edge | Coastal Retreats | 81

Munster | Co. Kerry

conservatory facing Dingle Harbour, and the gardens are wonderfully tended and colourful. In good weather, the deckchairs come out. Four of the ten rooms have sea views; the others look out on the garden. The decor is cosy and old-fashioned. Mark is very helpful with advice on the area. You're ensured a pleasant stay, but €65-85pps is on the steep side.

Out of the Blue

Waterside, Dingle, Co. Kerry
T: 066 915 0811 W: www.outoftheblue.ie
Opening Times: Closed Wed and Mar to mid-Nov
Directions: *[Map Ref. 14] On Dingle Harbour, opposite pier*
You know it's straight out of the sea because if there's no catch of the day, they don't open. Some of the best seafood you'll ever eat. No meat at all, so carnivores keep away. Tim Mason's deli and restaurant looks, on a sunny day, like something out of the Caribbean. It's bright blue outside, with simple pine chairs and tables, and yellow walls with naive paintings inside. One caveat: it's so jolly and simple, with menus chalked up on the blackboard, that you might think cheap 'n' cheerful. It ain't – count over €50 a head and make sure to book.

An Leath Phingin Eile

35 Main Street, Kenmare, Co. Kerry
T: 064 41559
Opening Times: Closed Mar and Tue; dinner only Wed-Mon
Directions: *[Map Ref. 15] Town centre*
A leath phingin is a halfpenny – you might remember its lovely Book of Kells-style design. This is replicated on the door of the restaurant, a premises previously occupied by another stalwart Kenmare restaurant, An Leath Phingin (hence the 'Eile'). Current owners Eddie and Gaelen Malcolmson used to own the acclaimed Linenmill restaurant in Westport. But enough history. This is one of the best places to eat in a seriously foodie town. Eddie uses local, mostly organic produce in French cooking with a modern twist. Highly imaginative starters (crab soufflé with hazelnut crust), unfussy mains (turbot with heavenly potato gratin) and sinful desserts (sticky toffee pudding). Prices as you'd expect on the West Coast (starters €9; mains €24). The rooms, upstairs and down, are cosy and cheerful, with lots of polished wood and open stone.

Munster | Co. Kerry

Kenmare at dusk

Brook Lane Hotel
Kenmare, Co. Kerry
T: 064 42077 W: www.brooklanehotel.com
Opening Times: Year round
Directions: *[Map Ref. 16] 5 minutes from Kenmare Town; take turn off for Sneem on Ring of Kerry road*

The Ring of Kerry is a wonderful place – it has golf, beaches, sensational views, and we love it. But it's mostly a jaunty, jolly, touristic place, especially attractive to young European cyclists and senior Irish golfers. You don't expect to find the kind of cool, understated boutique hotel that wouldn't be out of place in London's West End. Brook Lane Hotel has that low-key contemporary decor, subtle comfort and impeccable service that instantly reassures and relaxes. Prices from €65-150pps (for a suite in high season); this is great value, and no catch.

By the Water's Edge | Coastal Retreats | 83

Munster | Co. Kerry

D'Arcy's Oyster Bar and Guesthouse ⊗
Main Street, Kenmare, Co. Kerry
T: 064 41589 W: www.darcys.ie
Opening Times: Closed Mon in summer; weekends only, Oct-Apr
Directions: *[Map Ref. 17] Centre of town, top of Main Street*
D'Arcy's used to be a bank, and its well-proportioned, linen-tableclothed, mute-lit interior retains some of the mood of a serious counting house, but what's coming out of the till now are lobsters and oysters (live in a tank). Kick off with oysters accompanied by Bloody Mary granité – that will set you up for the escabeche of sea bream, followed by a whole lobster. Prices are perhaps a shade above the West Coast average (starters €10; mains €25; side dishes extra), but this is strong, confident cooking – serious enough to suit its surroundings. The seven rooms upstairs are discreet, tasteful, comfortable and, at €80pps, just a little overpriced.

Lime Tree Restaurant
Shelbourne Street, Kenmare, Co. Kerry
T: 064 41225 W: www.limetreerestaurant.com
Opening Times: Valentine's Day-Nov
Directions: *[Map Ref. 18] End of town beside Park Hotel*
In a converted nineteenth-century schoolhouse set back from the road, the Lime Tree is bright and airy within, with exposed stone walls and art for sale. Gary Fitzgerald is back as chef, and offers a varied menu. Start with mussels steamed with chorizo (€9.95) and move on to the fried hake with blue-cheese polenta (€23.95), or, for the vegetarians, poppy-seed blinis with goat's cheese and beetroot (€18.95). Adventurous fare, but the desserts are reassuringly trad: try the home-made ice cream with hot chocolate sauce (€7.95).

Mulcahy's Restaurant ⊗
36 Henry Street, Kenmare, Co. Kerry
T: 064 42383
Opening Times: Year round
Directions: *[Map Ref. 19] Town centre, top of Henry Street*
If you're getting sick of all the pan-fried fish (this is a coastal guide, after all), come to Bruce Mulcahy's spacious restaurant. The light, airy room is matched by light, subtle food. Bruce honed his skills in Japan and Thailand, and doesn't produce ubiquitous 'Asian fusion',

Munster | Co. Kerry

Park Hotel Kenmare

but the real thing: tempura, sushi, sashimi, but also – because he knows his customers – more trad dishes, like black sole and duck salad. It all works and it's all stodge- and grease-free. Set dinners €30 and €45.

Park Hotel Kenmare
Kenmare, Co. Kerry
T: 064 664 1220 W: www.parkkenmare.com
Opening Times: Mid-Apr to mid-Oct
Directions: *[Map Ref. 20] Top of town, overlooking bay*
We have a soft spot for this place – so big, jolly and Victorian – and the Park Hotel is particularly lucky in its location on Kenmare Bay. It's kept its nineteenth-century feel, with antiques, plush carpets, four-poster beds and chandeliers. The furnishings are beautiful, but can feel overburdened. However, the state-of-the-art spa,

By the Water's Edge | Coastal Retreats | 85

Munster | Co. Kerry

Sámas, is minimalist, clean, light, very twenty-first century and justly famous, though it maybe takes itself a bit seriously – €140 for a three-hour session and no booking in for one-off treatments. The nine deluxe suites and 24 junior suites all overlook Kenmare Bay. Service is excellent. You'll have a great stay, but you'll pay for it, with some of the highest rates in Ireland (€168-423pps). Like everyone else, they're making concessions to the recession, so check the website for special offers.

Shelburne Lodge €

Cork Road, Kenmare, Co. Kerry
T: 064 41013 **W:** www.shelburnelodge.com
Opening Times: Closed Dec-Feb
Directions: *[Map Ref. 21]* 250 metres outside Kenmare, on main Cork road

The extended Foley and O'Connell families own two well-loved restaurants in Kenmare, Packie's and the Purple Heather, as well as this eighteenth-century house in its own grounds. So Kenmare owes them a lot. Or vice versa. Spacious, stylish and laid-back, Shelburne Lodge is furnished in period detail, good value (B&B €50-85pps) and renowned for its breakfasts: not just fresh-squeezed orange juice, but apple juice; not just porridge, but porridge with whiskey cream. The nine rooms are divided between the main house and the nicely renovated coach house overlooking the tennis court.

Virginia's Guesthouse €

36 Henry Street, Kenmare, Co. Kerry
T: 064 41021 **W:** www.virginias-kenmare.com
Opening Times: Year round
Directions: *[Map Ref. 22]* Town centre, above Mulcahy's

It's above Mulcahy's (see entry), but separately run (though they do collaborate to offer interesting B&B-dining deals). Virginia's has eight cosy rooms, including family and triple rooms, not particularly big, but cheerfully furnished and good value (€30-50pps). This place wins out for cleanliness, friendliness, location and, for the breakfasts, beyond what you get in similar-priced B&Bs: porridge with whiskey cream, blue cheese over pears, and banana pancakes.

Munster | Co. Kerry

The Moorings €
Portmagee, Co. Kerry
T: 066 947 7108 W: www.themoorings.ie
Opening Times: Closed mid-Dec to mid-Jan
Directions: *[Map Ref. 23] On harbour, Portmagee*

Gerard and Patricia Kennedy have a guesthouse, bar/gastropub and restaurant under the one roof, and do a spanking trade. In summer, be prepared to wait, but they have the seeming-bedlam under control – turnover is fast. The Bridge bar serves food from noon-8.30pm and gets very lively in the evenings. The Moorings restaurant does oysters, lobster, mussels, scallops – all the usual seafood, and all fresh off a boat. It's good value, but this is the Ring of Kerry, so value means €50-60 a head including wine. Rooms at the guesthouse are well appointed, with attractive, unfussy decor, baths as well as showers, and reasonable value (€45-70pps). For views of Portmagee Harbour, ask for a deluxe sea-view room.

Parknasilla, Sneem

Munster | Co. Kerry

Aerial view of Parknasilla's stunning location, in Sneem

Parknasilla
Sneem, Co. Kerry
T: 064 45122 W: www.parknasillahotel.ie
Opening Times: Year round
Directions: [Map Ref. 24] 25 kilometres west of Kenmare

My friend's granny – a formidable matriarch – orders her entire extended family down to spend a long weekend at Parknasilla every

Munster | Co. Kerry

summer. It's that kind of place: old-school, Establishment, Bertie's favourite, which means it can be a bit uneven as to quality of rooms, service and food. Service is never rude, but sometimes 'relaxed'. Most people will forgive anything for those 300 acres of subtropical parkland overlooking Kenmare Bay and stunning sea or mountain views at every turn. All the front bedrooms have sea views – the Presidential, Princess Grace, Library and Penthouse suites have the best. Parknasilla is offering excellent recession deals: rooms from €80pps, even in high season. So book your extended family in now …

Tahilla Cove Country House

Tahilla Cove, Sneem, Co. Kerry
T: 064 664 5204 W: www.tahillacove.com
Opening Times: Closed mid-Oct to Easter
Directions: *[Map Ref. 25] Off N70, 5 miles east of Sneem, 11 miles west of Kenmare; signposted*

A cove is a wonderful thing when you're facing the Atlantic Ocean, and Tahilla Cove is one of the most benign and sheltered spots on the West Coast. The aptly named James and Deirdre Waterhouse have a house right on the water – their landscaped gardens go down to a private pier. The exterior is two houses, an attractive blend of art deco and Greek villa. Inside it's a bit floral and chintzy, but rooms are spacious and airy, and the atmosphere is relaxed. Seven of the rooms have sea views, and all of these have balconies/terraces (€75pps). Rooms without sea views are €15 cheaper.

Butler Arms

Waterville, Co. Kerry
T: 066 947 4144 W: www.butlerarms.com
Opening Times: Late Mar-late Oct
Directions: *[Map Ref. 26] Centre of Waterville, facing bay*

There's been a Butler Arms Hotel in Waterville for over 125 years, and it's been in the same family, the Huggards, for five generations. It contributed to the Ring of Kerry becoming a famed tourist destination. Everyone has stayed here, from Walt Disney to Catherine Zeta-Jones and, of course, Charlie Chaplin (spot the statue on the seafront). The hotel now has an old-fashioned feel and some of the rooms are dated in decor, but service remains exceptional. They are lovely to children and forbearing to serial

Munster | Co. Kerry

complainers. And the food is good, too. The sort of place you can imagine dowagers spending their summer months. Many of their 40 rooms have sea views – ask for a sea-view king executive. B&B €50-90pps.

Old Cable House €
Waterville, Co. Kerry
T: 066 947 4233 W: www.oldcablehouse.com
Opening Times: Year round
Directions: *[Map Ref. 27] Waterville Town, left turn near entrance to town, coming from Cahirciveen*

It's a big white Victorian house, built when the first transatlantic telephone cable was laid between Ireland and the United States. A housing estate has grown up close to it, but otherwise the location is good – close to the bay and town amenities. Rooms are clean and comfortable, though some are small. Breakfast, with scrambled eggs and locally smoked salmon, is good. B&B €30-35pps. Food in the restaurant is modern Irish, with emphasis on fish. Good value, especially the early dinner menu.

The Smugglers Inn
Cliff Road, Waterville, Co. Kerry
T: 066 947 4330 W: www.the-smugglers-inn.com
Opening Times: Mar-Nov
Directions: *[Map Ref. 28] On coast road beside golf course, coming from Cahirciveen direction*

It looks like a smuggler's inn, alright – standing alone off the road, facing a long, sandy, sometimes very wild beach – but there's nothing sinister about this charming restored farmhouse. This is right by Waterville's famed golf course, so it's the golfers' favourite and great for a drink after the game, but also has a lot of happy diners. The food, in the attractive conservatory dining room with views over Ballinskelligs Bay, is simple, solid, and tasty: Kerry lamb, John Dory, live lobsters and crayfish taken from a tank (set dinner €41; early dinner €30). Most of the rooms face the sea, but though they're not expensive (€50-75pps), they can be a bit cramped and could do with updating.

Munster | Co. Waterford

County Waterford

Introduction

The Waterford coastline is particularly dramatic, with a line of rugged mountains inland and to the north, many of which end in jagged cliffs right at the water's edge, with views across large, open bays. Interspersed are pretty, sandy bays – perfect for a picnic or day of sandcastle-building. Of these, Tramore is probably best known, although Dunmore East, Ardmore and Dungarvan are equally appealing. The Copper Coast (between Tramore and Dungarvan), the country's only EU and UNESCO Geopark, is well worth a detour for its stunning scenery, while the Hook Peninsula, dotted with ruins including the lovely Tintern Abbey, charming villages and an ancient lighthouse at its wildest tip, is a peaceful spot – perfect for birdwatching.

Munster | Co. Waterford

The Cliff House Hotel

Ardmore, Co. Waterford
T: 024 87800 W: www.thecliffhousehotel.com
Opening Times: Closed Jan to mid-Feb
Directions: *[Map Ref. 1] At end of Ardmore Village*

All 39 rooms in this smart new boutique hotel face the sea, thanks to a miracle of engineering: two buildings, hewn into the side of the cliff on Ardmore Bay, span seven levels. The suites (from €300 per room per night) are on two levels and have private verandas, where only the leaping dolphins (seriously) spy on you. If it's summer and/or you're hardy, you can walk down cedar steps to the rock pools for a sea bath. Otherwise, do a few lengths in the mosaic-

Munster | Co. Waterford

inlaid indoor pool. Head chef Martijn Kajuiter is Dutch, and has the height (6'8"), and the respect for Ireland and its resources to prove it. He uses kale and crabapples, makes soda-bread prune tart and avoids imported fish. His experimentation and wit have drawn comparison to Heston Blumenthal, and he can be precious about requests for low-grade condiments, like ketchup. Food is virtually dairy-free, so it's very light and clean, and you might even be able to manage all six courses (plus coffee, plus petits fours) of the tasting menu (€72.50). You'd come for the food or the location alone – the combination, with all those small details (Etro toiletries, Donegal tweed blankets on the beds and mosaic tiles in the bathrooms) make this one of the country's best weekend retreats.

Munster | Co. Waterford

White Horses Restaurant ✖ 🍴
Ardmore, Co. Waterford
T: 024 94040
Opening Times: Closed Mon; winter (Oct-Apr), open weekends only
Directions: *[Map Ref. 2] Centre of Ardmore Village*
The food in this small, bustling restaurant in the scenic village of Ardmore can hold its own with snazzy newcomer the Cliff House Hotel. The fish is so fresh it's leaping, the desserts, like banoffi and Mississippi mud pie, bring tears to the eyes, and vegetarians aren't forgotten. But the price is high – €9.50 for chowder! €32 for prawns in garlic butter? The food may be worth it, but the restaurant can be quite crowded at times, so get there early if you can. Low ceilings and wooden floors create a cosy, convivial atmosphere.

Cairbre House € 🏠
Dungarvan, Co. Waterford
T: 058 42338 **W:** www.cairbrehouse.com
Opening Times: Mid-Feb to mid-Nov
Directions: *[Map Ref. 3] Right exit off N25 at Strandside roundabout from Waterford; house 200 metres on left*
Staying in this ivy-clad Georgian guesthouse on the River Colligan, less than a mile from Dungarvan Harbour, is very comfortable and excellent value. The gardens are owner Brian Wickham's pride and joy, the en suite bedrooms look out on to Colligan Estuary, the decor throughout is warm and inviting, and breakfast is one of the best around, using herbs from the garden and offering a vegetarian option of fried courgettes, mushrooms and peppers on toast. From €42pps.

Quealy's Cafe Bar €
82 O'Connell Street, Dungarvan, Co. Waterford
T: 058 24555 **E:** quealysbarandrest@live.com
Opening Times: Closed Sun-Mon
Directions: *[Map Ref. 4] Just off main square, Dungarvan*
Andrew Quealy ran a successful restaurant, Q82, above his bar, but pre-empted the recession by moving to a bistro-style cafe bar in 2007. This is pub grub with a difference – imaginative, seasonal food (game in the winter, salads in the summer) and a choice of over 40 wines. Try the mixed seafood platter or the St. Tola goat's cheese with pine nuts.

Munster | Co. Waterford

Gaultier Lodge, Dunmore East, Co. Waterford

The Tannery

10 Quay Street, Dungarvan, Co. Waterford
T: 058 45420 **W:** www.tannery.ie
Opening Times: Year round
Directions: *[Map Ref. 5] Beside Old Market House on Lower Main Street*

According to legend, Paul Flynn's first two customers walked out when they read his menu. That was back in 1997; now Paul's crab crème brûlée is celebrated as far as New York. Located on the quayside in a former tannery, with an open kitchen and bright, wooden-floored, minimalist dining room, The Tannery serves traditional but experimental food at good prices (Crozier Blue soufflé and beetroot carpaccio €10.50, steamed lemon sole with mussel mousse €27.50, early-bird menu €30). This is the kind of place to which people make pilgrimages. Paul and wife Máire extended their empire last winter with the opening of the Tannery Cookery School in the guesthouse, the Tannery Townhouse, which is round the corner from the restaurant, on Church Street. The en suite rooms (from €60pps) are elegant and chic, and a continental breakfast is served in the room (no cooked breakfasts).

Munster | Co. Waterford

Beach Guesthouse €
Dunmore East, Co. Waterford
T: 051 383 316 W: www.dunmorebeachguesthouse.com
Opening Times: Closed Nov-Mar
Directions: *[Map Ref. 6] Dunmore East Village on seafront; approaching from Waterford City, keep left*
Recently built – and frankly, not wildly promising from the outside – Breda Battles' B&B wins out for value, friendliness, location and views, as well as airy, comfortable rooms and a good breakfast (buffet plus French toast, scrambled eggs, porridge, etc. made to order). Ask for one of the rooms at the front for a spectacular view to Hook Lighthouse. B&B €45pps, Jul-Aug; €40pps rest of the year.

Gaultier Lodge
Dunmore East, Co. Waterford
T: 051 382 549 W: www.gaultier-lodge.com
Opening Times: May-Nov
Directions: *[Map Ref. 7] From Waterford take R684, Dunmore East road, take left for Woodstown after 4 kilometres, right at beach; last house on left behind wall*
Three miles from Dunmore East and right on the beach at Woodstown Strand, this Georgian hunting lodge has private gardens and graceful period furniture in well-proportioned rooms painted cheerful colours. The views from the floor-to-ceiling windows stretch across to the Hook Peninsula. Sheila Molloy is an artist, and this goes for her cooking. Breakfast includes home-made scones and muffins, and she'll cook dinner on a day's notice. B&B from €65pps. Not suitable for small children, but dogs are welcome.

Rockett's of the Metal Man €
Westown, Tramore, Co. Waterford
T: 051 381 496 E: rockettsofthemetalman@eircom.net
Opening Times: Year round; phone to check off-season
Directions: *[Map Ref. 8] From Waterford, through Tramore*
This splendidly named pub is located on the summit of Westown Hill, with panoramic views of Tramore Bay. Very much the trad Irish pub – stone walls, pine fittings, an open brick fireplace and live sessions. The food is determinedly *Erin go Bragh*: colcannon, bacon and cabbage, spare ribs, crubeens (pig's trotters) and apple pie. All freshly made and very welcome on a wet and windy day.

Opposite: Sunset at Tramore Beach, Co. Waterford

Munster | Co. Waterford

Connaught

Connaught | Co. Galway

County Galway

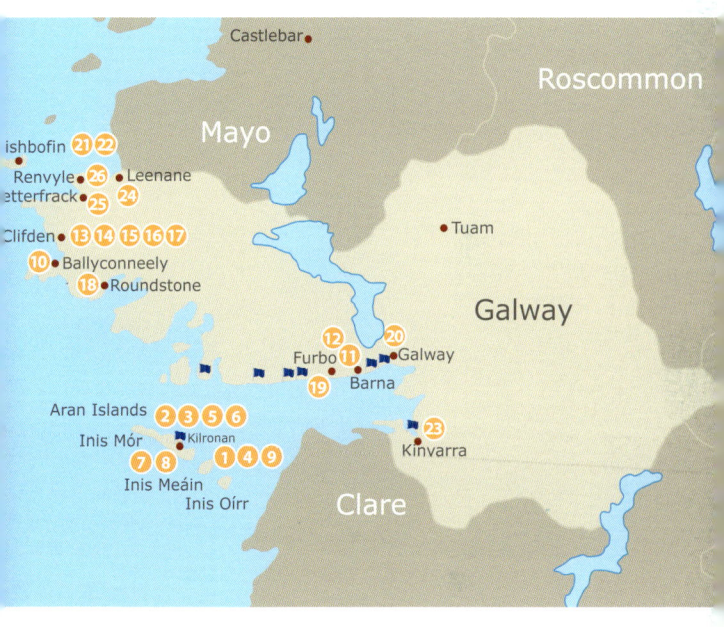

Introduction

With eight Blue Flag beaches and a series of windswept, isolated, romantic islands – as well as long stretches of mesmerising scenery – Galway is well served by the sea and coast. Take a tour of the north-west coast along the picturesquely named Sky Road, past Clifden Bay and Streamstown Bay. At the western end are Inishturk and Turbot islands, while Inishark and Inishbofin are visible from the pretty village of Cleggan. Connemara literally means 'inlets of the sea', and is a place where the tang of salt and cry of sea birds are never far off. Perhaps most magical of all are the Aran Islands, three rocky outcrops stuck out in the Atlantic Ocean that mark the very edge of Europe. Inis Mór, Inis Meáin and Inis Oírr each have their own distinctive atmosphere and character, but they share a unique and enduring appeal.

By the Water's Edge | Coastal Retreats | 99

Connaught | Co. Galway

The rocky outcrops of the Aran Islands

An Dún

Inis Meáin, Aran Islands, Co. Galway
T: 099 73047
Opening Times: Closed Dec-Feb
Directions: *[Map Ref. 1] Centre of island, beside John Millington Synge Museum*

Even without the aromatherapy treatments, this place offers spa-quality relaxation by virtue of its stunning location. At the foot of Dun Conchubhar and by the water's edge on the tranquil Inis Meáin. Pop next door to the John Millington Synge Museum for a bit of cultural history or stroll to the thatched pub for some local history. Don't miss the chowder in the cafe, which has a charming outdoor terrace. Try the restaurant for simple but delicious home-

Connaught | Co. Galway

made food. Think seafood, roast rack of lamb and freshly baked tarts. Set three-course menu €25-30. The decor is country-comfy, and the extension to the original cottage has brought space, light and sea views in abundance. The five en suite rooms are comfortably furnished (€45-50pps).

Aran Islands Hotel

Kilronan, Inis Mór, Aran Islands, Co. Galway
T: 099 61104 W: www.aranislandshotel.com
Opening Times: Closed 20-28 Dec
Directions: *[Map Ref. 2] Kilronan Harbour, Aranmore*
This recently refurbished hotel overlooks Kilronan Harbour. Its bar, Paitin Jack's, is a hub for locals, who may well start up an impromptu céilí. Decor-wise, it's curl-up cosy – think wooden furniture, stone walls and open fires. There is decent bar food to be had in Paitin Jack's and great seafood in the restaurant, which has cracking sea views. The bedrooms are spacious and warm, in a thickly-carpeted-and-pine-furniture sort of way. Family rooms are large and will comfortably sleep six. All are en suite. Five of the rooms have views over the harbour and access to a communal balcony, which can be a little off-putting. Request Room 100 for the best sea view. High season €69pps; €10 weekend supplement per person per night.

Fisherman's Cottage

Inis Oírr, Aran Islands, Co. Galway
T: 099 75073 W: www.southaran.com
Opening Times: Closed Mon (Nov-Mar)
Directions: *[Map Ref. 3] Right at pier, 300 metres along*
There are moments on Inis Oírr when you can hear your own heart beating. Take a break from the silence and engage in some foodie chat at this quaint restaurant with rooms. Owners Maria and Enda Conneely are evangelical about slow food, and it shows in their cooking of local seafood and meat dishes (€14-20). The cottage is picture-postcard pretty, with whitewashed walls and aqua-blue sills. Even the rickety blue furniture in the cosy dining room is adorable. There are four en suite rooms (€40pps; €45 single occupancy) with trusty iron beds, crisp white linen, more whitewash and stunning sea views. Sit in the garden, admire the wildflowers, look out to sea, and feel glad to be alive. Yoga, cookery and language classes are also available.

Connaught | Co. Galway

Inis Meáin Restaurant and Suites

Inis Meáin, Aran Islands, Co. Galway
T: 086 826 6026 **W:** www.inismeain.com
Opening Times: May-Aug
Directions: *[Map Ref. 4] Past only pub on left, take next right, then first left*

Stark and beautiful, with a low stature shaped like a windbreaking beach hut. The restaurant interior involves stylish olive-green leather banquet seating, dark wood and stone. Any austerity is softened by the light from the amazing window, which runs the length of the dining room and gives panoramic views of the ocean. Take a seat and enjoy the speciality – baked lobster (€35), served with vegetables from the garden. Lay your head down in one of three stylish suites with simple themes of wood, stone and glass. Each has uninterrupted sea views. The minibar is very smart – think Green & Black's chocolate and champagne. No TV. A slice of heaven, albeit at a price (€125pps; €62 single supplement; minimum stay of two nights).

A suite at Inis Meáin Restaurant and Suites, Aran Islands

Connaught | Co. Galway

Kilmurvey House
Inis Mór, Aran Islands, Co. Galway
T: 099 61218 W: www.irelandwide.com/acom/kilmurveyhouse
Opening Times: Closed 31 Oct-1 Apr
Directions: *[Map Ref.5] 7 kilometres from Kilronan (minibus from harbour)*
Dating back to the eighteenth century, this historic stone-walled house was once the seat of the 'Ferocious O'Flahertys', who sound like trouble. Four miles from Kilronan, at the base of the majestic Dun Aengus, this is an isolated interlude from everyday worries. The grand old house has plenty of original features, but isn't crazily plush. The decor is homely, if a tad fussy. En suite bedrooms (€45-50pps) in the new wing are stylish, bright and extremely large, with views across the island and towards the water. Try the cinnamon French toast for breakfast before setting out on an archaeological expedition. Return for a dinner of local catch, vegetables from the garden and a bottle of wine from the cellar (three courses €25-30). If dinner is not being served, they will kindly ferry you to Kilronan. Five-minute walk to the beach.

Mainistir House Hotel
Inis Mór, Aran Islands, Co. Galway
T: 099 61169
Opening Times: Year round
Directions: *[Map Ref.6] From harbour, a mile along main road*
If the words 'hostel' or 'dorm' curdle your cappuccino, this is not the place for you. On the other hand, if you are looking for a cheap, pleasant option, this could be it. The dormitories and private rooms are quite pretty, very clean and individually decorated around a sea theme. The biggest selling point is the panoramic view of the ocean. There is an all-you-can-eat vegetarian buffet on offer in the evenings (€15; bring your own wine). The classical music in the dining room is a little loud and gets on your wick – a bit like those madcap Italians at the next table maybe. This isn't luxury, but it's a very good hostel, and excellent value. Dorms €18pps. Private rooms €50pps.

Man of Aran Cottages
Kilmurvey, Inis Mór, Aran Islands, Co. Galway
T: 099 61301 W: www.manofarancottage.com
Opening Times: Mar-Oct
Directions: *[Map Ref.7] 6.5 kilometres from Kilronan (minibus available)*

Connaught | Co. Galway

Connemara, Co. Galway

Americans flock to this quaint B&B – if you recognise that thatched roof, it was built as part of the *Man of Aran* set. Aside from its celluloid history and straw roof, the location is amazing – imagine looking out over the Atlantic through fields of wildflowers, vegetables and herbs. The Man of Aran cottages are situated four miles from Kilronan Pier and offer three small rooms (only one is en suite). Because these are cottages, ceilings are low and interiors rustic. Enjoy a dinner of salmon, monkfish or roast lamb, accompanied by a salad of mixed leaves and flowers from the garden (three-course menu €35). En suite room €45pps; €15 single supplement. Dinner, residents only; credit cards not accepted.

Pier House

Kilronan, Inis Mór, Aran Islands, Co. Galway
T: 099 61417 W: www.pierhousearan.com
Opening Times: Mid-Mar to mid-Oct
Directions: *[Map Ref. 8] 50 metres from ferry point, overlooking pier*

& **Connaught** | Co. Galway

Hustle and bustle is rare on the Aran Islands, but rush hour hits Kilronan Pier when the ferries dock. As the name suggests, Pier House is a very short scramble and is constantly busy. Rooms at the front have views of the sea, and those at the back look out on the stone-walled Aran landscape. Not a bad deal either way. All are en suite. The guesthouse interior is comfy, rather than fancy. The on-site restaurant is leased out – emphasis is on seafood, but the quality of food can be up and down. Good seating area at the front of the B&B to enjoy the beautiful harbour view. B&B €60pps; €10 single supplement.

Tig Congaile
Moore Village, Inis Meáin, Aran Islands, Co. Galway
T: 099 73085
Opening Times: Closed Oct-Easter
Directions: *[Map Ref. 9] Moore Village; five-minute walk from pier*
You'll spot Tig Congaile on the choppy approach to Inis Meáin. This popular B&B and restaurant is an imposing, well-maintained, pale yellow house on a hill, with views towards Clare and the Cliffs of Moher. It's a five-minute walk from the pier, and run by Vilma and Padric Conneely. Their foodie philosophy is to use ingredients that are steadfastly organic, local and, where possible, from the sea. Try the sea-vegetable soup and get a lifetime of essential minerals in one bowl. For dinner try the steak (€14-21) or half-lobster (€17). Tig Congaile's decor is uncluttered, wooden, modern, bright and clean. En suite rooms (€40pps) are a good size, with stunning sea views from rooms 3, 4 and 7 in particular.

Mannin Bay Hotel
Ballyconneely, Connemara, Galway
T: 095 23120 **W:** www.manninbayhotel.com
Opening Times: Mar-5 Jan
Directions: *[Map Ref. 10] 8 kilometres from Clifden Town, beside Connemara Golf Links*
Don't be put off by the salmon colour on the new-build exterior. This luxury country house hotel boasts a killer location overlooking Mannin Bay. It is also within walking distance of some beautiful beaches and five miles outside Clifden. On a good day, you may even spot a colony of seals. Great family value to be found with the two-room suite, which includes sea views, dining and sitting areas, plus a couple of flat-screen TVs. The decor in the bedrooms is

Connaught | Co. Galway

modern, with neutral colour schemes of white and cream. The restaurant has great views of the water and offers a good selection of seafood. Unfortunately, the dining room looks like a function room and the bar area is a bit dull. On the upside, it's very relaxed and staff are super-helpful. From €60pps.

O Grady's on the Pier ⊗
Seapoint, Barna, Co. Galway
T: 091 592 223 W: www.ogradysonthepier.com
Opening Times: Year round; bookings from 3pm
Directions: *[Map Ref. 11] Seapoint Pier, overlooking bay*
The place to be on a stormy Galway afternoon. Sip an aperitif and watch the waves roar towards the windows. The pub-style interior, with open turf fire and laid-back seafaring theme, makes this a popular joint with hungry tourists and protective locals, but really, it's the delicate cooking of seafood and daily blackboard specials that keep the crowds coming. Owner Michael O Grady aims to let the seafood speak for itself, as far as possible, but innovation is evident, with scallops and black pudding dishes, or skate wing and white-bait tempura. Don't worry – meat-eaters are catered for as well. Fabulous outdoor seating area for when the sun shines. Lunch and dinner served; booking advised for Fridays, Saturdays and other peak times.

The Twelve
Barna Village, Galway
T: 091 597 000 W: www.thetwelvehotel.ie
Opening Times: Year round
Directions: *[Map Ref. 12] On right-hand side of crossroads as you enter Barna*
This place has put the bling into Barna. Think champagne bar, a chef's table and some very modern decor – The Twelve has all the trappings of a big city hang-out that got lost in the wilds of Connemara. Bedrooms are large (B&B €80pps), and some come with a mini kitchen/bar, flat-screen TV, iPod docking station and double jacuzzi for extra sass. There's good casual dining in The Pins bar, with home-made breads, pastries, gourmet pizza, salads and hot dishes on offer. The decor is pleasant, with dark wood softened by low lighting, comfy sofas and an open fire. You'll find fine dining upstairs in West Restaurant, with all the usual seafood and meat options, plus a hugely extensive wine list.

Connaught | Co. Galway

The Twelve, Barna Village

Ardagh Hotel and Restaurant

Ballyconneely Road, Clifden, Co. Galway
T: 095 21384 W: www.ardaghhotel.com
Opening Times: Mar-Nov
Directions: *[Map Ref. 13] 3 kilometres from Clifden on Ballyconneely Road*

A bit '70s on the outside, but think country chic on the inside: open fires, plenty of sink-in sofas, candles on every surface and a very relaxed ambience. Enjoy a few quiet drinks in the bar, then try a dinner of wild Connemara smoked salmon (€15.50) or quail (€14.50) to start, followed by turbot (€29.50) or black Dover sole on the bone (€39.50). The dining-room decor isn't very appealing – more of a breakfast room or jaded country kitchen in vibe – but it has a spectacular view of the water. Watch the mesmerising light changes over Ardbear Bay. Some of the furniture needs a bit of TLC, but bedrooms are three-star standard, spacious, bright and comfortable, with blue, green and gold hues. Superior room with a sea view, B&B €65pps.

By the Water's Edge | Coastal Retreats

Connaught | Co. Galway

Dolphin Beach House
Lower Sky Road, Clifden, Co. Galway
T: 095 21204 W: www.dolphinbeachhouse.com
Opening Times: Year round
Directions: *[Map Ref. 14] 4.5 kilometres from Clifden on Sky Road; keep left at fork, take lower Sky Road*
Take the Sky Road out of Clifden to find this gem of a getaway with beautiful views of Dolphin Bay. The colour scheme in the new part of the house calls to mind a Spanish hacienda, yet the decorative woodwork and glass lends a Scandinavian vibe. Turf fires burn most days in the sitting room, which is part of the original old-beamed cottage, and the family dogs lap up attention from guests. There are nautical touches throughout. Great food is served in a breakfast room with a panoramic backdrop. Each bedroom has its own personality, with mosaics, hand-carved mirrors, sleigh beds and amazing home-made headboards. Downstairs bedrooms have terraces that lead down to the cove. Just what the doc ordered for major stress relief. Dinner available on request (€40); B&B €65-90pps.

Mallmore Country House
Ballyconneely Road, Clifden, Co. Galway
T: 095 21460 W: www.mallmorecountryhouse.com
Opening Times: Year round
Directions: *[Map Ref. 15] 2 kilometres from Clifden; signposted off Ballyconneely Road*
This eighteenth-century house, on the shores of Clifden Bay, is steeped in history and character. Original residents, the D'Arcy family, built Clifden to give employment to the local population. The house sits on 35 acres of beautiful mature woodland and has its own Connemara ponies. Grab a book and sink into the comfortable settee by the turf fire, or the armchairs by the huge windows, and enjoy the view of the bay. The bedrooms are large and bright, with splashes of dynamic wallpaper, pretty upholstery and billowing drapes. Breakfast is substantial and varied. Bedrooms have DVD players – great for a rainy day. Climb under the duvet and dream of Mr D'Arcy, or bring your own. B&B €40pps.

Dolphin Beach House, Lower Sky Road, Clifden

Connaught | Co. Galway

Connaught | Co. Galway

The Quay House
Beach Road, Clifden, Co. Galway
T: 095 21369 W: www.thequayhouse.com
Opening Times: Mid-Mar to end Oct
Directions: *[Map Ref. 16] Town centre, overlooking harbour; follow signs for Beach Road*

The Quay House is Clifden's oldest building, and has had a few identity crises – previous incarnations include the harbourmaster's house, a monastery and a convent. These days, it's a colonial-style townhouse. Paddy and Julia Foyle have magicked the harbourside building into something very different to any average B&B. On arrival, you are greeted by two huge elephant tusks in the hallway and tiger skins on the back of the settee. It's all quite wacky. Bedrooms are large and beautifully decorated in different styles, with romantic four-poster beds, enormous gilded mirrors, or a few bits of African roadkill dotted here and there. The Napoleon and African rooms have the best views of the harbour. Breakfast is served in a quirky and pretty conservatory. B&B €60-75pps.

Mitchell's Restaurant
Market Street, Clifden, Connemara, Co. Galway
T: 095 21867
Opening Times: Mid-Feb to end Oct
Directions: *[Map Ref. 17] Town centre, beside SuperValu*

Mitchell's Restaurant, in the centre of Clifden, is a family-run goldmine. The dining room, with its exposed stonework, wooden tables, oil lamps and old bar counter, has a very rustic feel. The menu is a total crowd-pleaser – perfect for a thriving tourist town. Drop by for lunch, and you'll find sandwiches, home-made soups and freshly baked bread, as well as hot daily specials. Dinner involves some seafood options, a good steak and more traditional Irish cuisine, like bacon and cabbage (three-course dinner €27.50). There's also a children's menu during the day. Weekend booking advised.

The Anglers Return
Roundstone, Connemara, Toombeola, Co. Galway
T: 095 31091 W: www.anglersreturn.com
Opening Times: End Feb to end Nov
Directions: *[Map Ref. 18] From Galway, N59 towards Clifden, left on R341 towards Roundstone for 4 miles; house on left*

Connaught | Co. Galway

The Anglers Return, Connemara

A quaint and tranquil eighteenth-century house with a stunning location on the Ballynahinch River. Trout-fishing is a huge attraction here, but those left cold by its charms will also find plenty of beautiful beaches, nature walks and gardens to explore round about. Inside, the house is unfussy, arty and country-style, with plenty of original features, antiques, neutral walls, a turf fire and lazing-around furniture. Bedrooms are pared-back pretty, with mahogany beds, dressing tables, vases of wildflowers from the garden and crisp white linen. Not all rooms are en suite, so be sure to check. For stunning coastal views ask for the Lascelles Room when booking. An artist's haven. B&B €98pps.

Connemara Coast Hotel

Furbo, Galway, Co. Galway
T: 091 592 108 W: www.connemaracoast.ie
Opening Times: Year round
Directions: *[Map Ref. 19]* 9 kilometres from Galway on Spiddal road
The Connemara Coast Hotel is an institution. Its location on the water is spectacular, and many local weddings and celebrations take place here. In recent years, the hotel has started to show a little wear and tear in the bedrooms, but a gradual refurbishment is addressing this problem. The communal areas are bright and offer

Connaught | Co. Galway

plenty of places to sit and relax by the fire or play a game of chess. The bar is a little small for the hotel, particularly noticable at weekends, when locals drop by for the music. Bedrooms are a good size and simply but contemporarily decorated with velvet-soft furnishings. While en suites are on the small side, this isn't a deal-breaker. Try an executive suite for great sea views, king-size bed and complimentary decanter of sherry (€155pps). Leisure facilities are decent, with a great pool and a kids' club, and the outdoor hot tub certainly deserves a try-out. The pub grub is typical but good, while the restaurant serves seafood and hearty meat dishes. An easygoing country-type hotel – portions are large, just like the welcome.

The Heron's Rest
Longwalk, Spanish Arch, Galway
T: 091 539 574 W: www.theheronsrest.com
Opening Times: Apr-Dec
Directions: *[Map Ref. 20] Longwalk, near Spanish Arch*
Sorcha Molloy's quirky 'boutique B&B' has a no-sausage policy, so if your favourite morning meal is a breakfast roll, don't book a room. However, if home-made muffins, polenta cakes, peppered mackerel, smoked salmon and sweet vanilla omelettes tick all the right boxes, then do. Breakfast is served on a big old eight-seater oak table, while Sorcha cooks and chats with the guests. The house has views over Claddagh Harbour, the River Corrib and out towards the sea. Bedrooms are quite intimate, but uniquely decorated with brightly coloured throws and soft white linen. The en suite master bedroom has a gorgeous sea view. It is a five-minute walk past the Spanish Arch and the ubiquitous bongo drummers to get to Quay Street, where all the action happens. Parking is pay and display. B&B €75pps.

The Dolphin Hotel and Restaurant
Inishbofin Island, Co. Galway
T: 095 45991 W: www.dolphinhotel.ie
Opening Times: Mar-Nov
Directions: *[Map Ref. 21] Take boat from Cleggan Pier*
A cool and eco-friendly addition to the island, the dark brick and wood exterior complements the wild Inishbofin landscape, and while the interior is fairly sparse, it's welcoming, with plenty of windows and natural light. All of the neutrally decorated upstairs

Rosleague Manor Hotel, Letterfrack

Connaught | Co. Galway

bedrooms have sea views, and the three on the ground floor have sundecks. Beyond all the *Grand Designs* talk is the food, which is renowned. At lunch, everything from bread to ice cream is home-made. The evening menu matures well to include seafood, meat and a vegetarian option. The dining room is extremely bright, with wooden features and glass to enjoy the breathtaking view. Two nights' B&B with one dinner €175-199pps.

Doonmore Hotel
Inishbofin Island, Co. Galway
T: 095 45804/14 **W:** www.doonmorehotel.com
Opening Times: Mar-Oct
Directions: *[Map Ref. 22] Take boat from Cleggan Pier*
An old-style hotel that's unafraid to let its hair down; the bar is famous for its traditional music sessions and congenial atmosphere. It also has a seafaring vibe, with panoramic views over the Atlantic Ocean, and an authentic nautical theme. Cosy, with low ceilings and turf fires, the bar is more like a sitting room and is a decent spot for a quick bite or casual seafood dinner in the restaurant. A napkin-in-glass kind of place. Bedrooms aren't plush, but they're a good size, fairly neutrally decorated, homely and with great sea views (B&B €75pps). The hotel is very family-friendly, and staff make us feel like nothing is too much trouble.

Connaught | Co. Galway

Rosleague Manor Hotel

Letterfrack, Co. Galway
T: 095 41101 **W:** www.rosleague.com
Opening Times: Mid-Mar to Nov
Directions: *[Map Ref. 25] 11 kilometres from Clifden on N59*

A romantic manor on the shores of Ballinakill Bay, coloured pink and accessorised with ivy. This elegant regency hotel is set on 30 acres of woodland and is popular for small weddings. There are log fires aplenty, two old-world drawing rooms and antiques around every corner – you need a brandy to fit in. Cleggan lobster and Connemara lamb are the restaurant specialities. The dining room has views of the gardens and the water. It's a classy country-manor affair, with polished mahogany furniture, chandeliers and historical paintings. Bedrooms are lovely, with brass or four-poster beds, sturdy period furniture, soft drapes and sea views to the front. €85-125pps; set-menu dinner €50.

Renvyle House Hotel

Renvyle, Connemara, Co. Galway
T: 095 43511 **W:** www.renvyle.com
Opening Times: Closed Dec (except Christmas), mid-Jan to mid-Feb
Directions: *[Map Ref. 26] 18 kilometres north of Clifden*

This, the former home of Oliver St. John Gogarty, was also a playground for Yeats, Lady Gregory and Churchill. Mementos of their time here are dotted around the historic country house. Its location, on the shores of the Atlantic, is deliciously remote and makes you wish for the perfect storm. You can't help but snuggle by the turf fire in the long lounge. Decent bar food and lunches are served in the plant-filled conservatory. The restaurant's dining room is bright and pleasant, with copper pots hanging over a fireplace. Choose from beef, lamb, game and seafood. Food is a little heavy on the sauce, but delicious despite. Rise for breakfast to try the eggs Benedict and Guinness potato cakes. Some bedrooms need a dash of TLC – think pine furniture and bottle-green carpet – while others are Big House luxurious. Bag numbers 19 or 20 for the best views. B&B and dinner €155pps.

Connaught | Co. Mayo

County Mayo

Introduction

Jutting out into the wild Atlantic Ocean, Mayo is an excitingly rugged, unspoiled spot – sparsely populated, but particularly rich in natural beauty. The shoreline is carved into a series of spectacular inlets and bays, hollowed out by the sometimes savage sea. Off the Mullet Peninsula, on the north side of Mayo, is the country's largest island, lovely Achill. Here you will find some of Europe's highest cliffs, as well as Blue Flag beaches, megalithic tombs and the poignant deserted villages of Slievemore and Ailt. Elly Bay has lovely beaches, while Clare Island – at the mouth of Clew Bay and forever synonymous with pirate queen Grace O'Malley – has the remains of a fifteenth-century Cistercian friary.

By the Water's Edge | Coastal Retreats | 115

Connaught | Co. Mayo

The Bervie, Keel, Achill Island

Achill Cliff House Hotel
Keel, Achill Island, Co. Mayo
T: 098 43400 **W:** www.achillcliff.com
Opening Times: Year round
Directions: *[Map Ref. 1] Facing Keel Strand, Achill Island*
Ask for rooms at the front, facing Keel Beach – 11 and 12 are the best. Expect clean, comfortable rooms, well-sprung mattresses and value for money (€50-80pps). Don't expect top luxury, though there is a sauna. The set menu in the restaurant is amazingly reasonable (€26.50 for three courses), but all the good fish dishes are à la carte, and in Achill, you really want to be ordering fish. Unusually for the area, it's open all year round.

The Beehive
Keel, Achill Island, Co. Mayo
T: 098 43134
Opening Times: 9.30am-6pm
Directions: *[Map Ref. 2] Centre of Keel Village, on main road through Achill*

Connaught | Co. Mayo

The adventurous are eating nettle soup, and showing off how delicious they find it. Everyone else is guzzling chowder and looking forward to banoffi. Basking sharks are swimming into Keel Strand. You're on Achill Island – half of it is tourist hell and the other half is sublime. You'll definitely stop here, at Michael and Patricia Joyce's craft shop and cafe, and you won't be disappointed.

The Bervie

Keel, Achill Island, Co. Mayo
T: 098 43114 W: www.bervieachill.com
Opening Times: Easter-Nov
Directions: *[Map Ref. 3] Overlooking Keel Strand; signposted from village*

The situation, on the south-facing beach of Keel, and John and Elizabeth Barrett's excellent hospitality keep guests returning to The Bervie. A former coastguard station, the building is long, white, attractive, and fits comfortably into the stunning landscape. Elizabeth was born here, which gives a nice sense of continuity. Half of the 14 en suite rooms (€50-60pps) overlook Clew Bay. Room 17 has the best view. Dinner, cooked by Elizabeth, is traditional and moreish – €45 for a five-course dinner, and you pay less for fewer courses.

Mary's

Main Street, Ballycastle, Co. Mayo
T: 096 43361
Opening Times: Summer, 10am-6pm; closed Sun (Oct-Easter) and first three weeks Jan
Directions: *[Map Ref. 4] Main Street, Ballycastle*

Mary Munnelly is a great cook who provides breakfast, lunch and afternoon tea in her cosy stone-fronted cottage. She knows her worth, so quiche is €10.90 and a ham sandwich €10.50, but the pastry is wonderfully light, the ham thickly sliced off the bone, and the bread home-made. Only the truly neurotic would refuse the cakes. You can glimpse the sea from the garden round the back. Cash only.

Stella Maris Country House Hotel

Ballycastle, Co. Mayo
T: 096 43322 W: www.stellamarisireland.com
Opening Times: Closed Oct-Apr

Connaught | Co. Mayo

Stella Maris Country House Hotel, Ballycastle

Directions: *[Map Ref. 5] 1.5 miles west of Ballycastle Village; signposted*

The Stella Maris ticks every box, whether you're on a romantic weekend, family break or trying to write the great Irish novel. The long white building was a nineteenth-century coastguard headquarters, so it faces out to the Atlantic, with stunning, scary views of Downpatrick Head. The addition of a 100-foot-long conservatory allows you to admire that rugged view from a sunlounger. Food by chef-proprietor Frances Kelly is imaginative French-meets-Irish, with locally sourced ingredients. There are just 12 rooms (€112.50pps), of which ten are ocean-facing, so book ahead and look forward to the full country house treatment.

Ardmore Country House and Restaurant

The Quay, Westport, Co. Mayo
T: 098 25994 W: www.ardmorecountryhouse.com
Opening Times: Closed Jan-Feb
Directions: *[Map Ref. 6] Off Louisburgh coast road, 3 kilometres from Westport Town*

You'd stay here for the views across Clew Bay. It's also comfortable, hospitable, brightly furnished and family run. Just 13 rooms, seven with views (ask for numbers 103, 104, 105 or 106). Breakfast is great: a lovely, non-greasy version of the full Irish, as well as fresh fruit, home-made bread and a fish plate. B&B from €75pps, but if you stay four nights, the price goes down. The restaurant overlooking the bay is large enough to welcome non-residents. Pat Hoban's food is no-nonsense trad: black pudding with apple compote, roast duckling with Grand Marnier, and the competitively priced set menu (€35) is excellent value.

Connaught | Co. Mayo

Cabot's Source@The Linen Mill ❌ €
The Demesne, Westport, Co. Mayo
T: 098 50546 W: www.cabotssource.com
Opening Times: 6pm-10pm (dinner only)
Directions: *[Map Ref. 7] Westport Town, off Newport Road*
Now in new, larger premises in the Linen Mill, Cabot's Source was one of the culinary events in Westport when it opened last year. This is seriously good food at good prices. As the name suggests, owner Redmond Cabot is passionate about sourcing locally, and chef Martin is all about flair and simplicity. Try the poached pear and blue cheese salad (€7.50) for starters, then dive into a succulent T-bone steak (€27). The most expensive main pasta dishes are around €13.

Cronin's Sheebeen ❌ €
Rosbeg, Westport, Co. Mayo
T: 098 26528 W: www.croninssheebeen.com
Opening Times: Year round
Directions: *[Map Ref. 8] Westport Harbour*
Last year, this thatched whitewashed pub overlooking Clew Bay got into the Michelin guide, as one of the 17 best eating-out pubs in Ireland. We're not surprised, and neither are the locals – owners Simon and Colm Cronin and head chef Frankie Mallon respect their great local produce by keeping it simple. Chowder (€5.50) is as good as anywhere; potted salmon (€7.50), a great, old-fashioned dish, while Thai lamb curry (€13.50) or, in the winter, peppered venison (€20.50) provide imaginative alternatives to fish. Food this good at these prices means it can be hard getting a table in summer.

The Lemon Peel €
The Octagon, Westport, Co. Mayo
T: 098 26929 W: www.lemonpeel.ie
Opening Times: Closed Mon; ring in advance off-season
Directions: *[Map Ref. 9] Town centre, between Octagon and Church Lane*
Robbie McMenamin migrated briefly to the harbour, but his customers wanted him back in the centre, round the corner from Matt Molloy's. They got their way – McMenamin's returned to his small, friendly restaurant with an excellently priced, varied menu. Try the Lemon Peel salad with feta cheese (€8), and you cannot go wrong with the stuffed roast pork and apple and brandy sauce (€18).

Connaught | Co. Mayo

McGing's
High Street, Westport, Co. Mayo
T: 098 29743
Opening Times: Year round
Directions: *[Map Ref. 10] Off The Octagon, Westport*
Westport is one of the great pubbing towns, and we don't like to pick and choose between its watering holes, but since Matt Molloy's (of Chieftains fame) gets the most publicity, we're advancing the cause of McGing's. It's one of those plainly furnished, tile-floored, low-ceilinged pubs – nothing fancy, no hint of olde worlde, but rocking. Great sessions – not just trad, but jazz and blues and a cool crowd.

Park Inn Mulranny
Mulranny, Westport, Co. Mayo
T: 098 36000 W: www.parkinnmulranny.ie
Opening Times: Year round
Directions: *[Map Ref. 11] Mulranny Village, N59 from Westport to Bangor Ellis*
Big, cheerful and late Victorian, like all the former Great Western Hotels. The Park Inn Mulranny reopened in 2005 and now offers relaxed four-star luxury (pool and jacuzzi) in a five-star location. You're close to Achill Island and overlooking a Blue Flag beach, with views of Croagh Patrick. Twenty of the rooms have a sea view (nab the John Lennon Suite for extra luxury and a panoramic vista). Especially good for families and, with prices starting at €55pps, great value for everyone. The food in either the Nephin Restaurant or the bar is the second talking point (after the location) because you'll get foie gras, wild venison or soy and ginger tofu – classy/adventurous fare that the kitchen pulls off. Be warned: staff can be flighty ...

View from the Park Inn Mulranny

Connaught | Co. Sligo

County Sligo

Introduction

Sligo has always been inexorably linked with the sea – its name comes from the Irish *Sligeach*, or 'shelly place', and there are a host of sandy beaches here. The best are to be found in the area around Enniscrone, which has views of some of the best sunsets along the West Coast. Sligo's coastline also reflects a sad side to Irish history, that of the Great Famine, and a museum near Dromore West (Culkin's Emigration Museum) stands on the site of a nineteenth-century emigration agency, where thousands of Irish left to seek a new life in the New World. Sligo, of course, is also Yeats country, and visitors can follow in the footsteps of one of Ireland's greatest poets by visiting the 'Lake Isle of Innisfree' at Lough Gill in the north of the county, near Sligo Town.

By the Water's Edge | Coastal Retreats

Connaught | Co. Sligo

Radisson SAS Hotel and Spa, Ballincar, Rosses Point

Radisson SAS Hotel and Spa
Ballincar, Rosses Point, Co. Sligo
T: 071 914 0008 W: www.radissonsas.com
Opening Times: Year round
Directions: *[Map Ref. 1] 2 miles from Sligo Town in direction of Rosses Point*

Not the most appealing exterior, but a comfortable, light-filled, well-staffed hotel with a superb location between Ben Bulben and Sligo Bay. You can't really go wrong with the views, but ask for suites 317 or 319 – or any of the corner suites – for a panorama of sea with a balcony. There's a pool in the leisure centre if you can't face the icy brine. You can pay as little as €40pps off-season, but suites on summer weekends are €125pps.

Connaught | Co. Sligo

The Waterfront €
Rosses Point, Co. Sligo
T: 071 917 7122
Opening Times: Year round; phone to check off-season
Directions: *[Map Ref. 2] Rosses Point, on waterfront*
Sligo Town has two seaside suburbs: to the west, Strandhill, for the surfers, and to the north, Rosses Point, for the golfers. Both suit everyone who wants to swim, walk or watch the sunset – which, in summer, is most Sligo locals and all the tourists. Joe Grogan's bar is right on the waterfront in Rosses Point. Food (from 5pm; no lunch) is mussels, oysters, catch of the day and pizzas. It's busy, so get there early.

Bella Vista Bar and Bistro €
Shore Road, Strandhill, Co. Sligo
T: 071 912 2222 W: www.bellavista.ie
Opening Times: Year round
Directions: *[Map Ref. 3] Strandhill, on seafront*
Strandhill is younger, hipper and more laid-back than Rosses Point. The aptly named Bella Vista is more or less on the beach, and is a large, busy, cheerful place, all pine wood and potted plants. The terrace outside is good in sunny weather. Expect soup, toasties, pasta and pizzas at lunch, and steaks and fish at dinner. Good, plain cooking, good atmosphere and good value.

The Beach Bar/Aughris House €
Aughris Head, Templeboy, Co. Sligo
T: (Bar) 071 917 6465; (Rooms) 071 916 6703
W: www.thebeachbarsligo.com
Opening Times: Food served weekends only
Directions: *[Map Ref. 4] Off N59, on coast road to Aughris Head*
It's well off the beaten track (and prepare to get in conversation with a surfer with a thousand-yard stare), but the Beach Bar is *right* on the beach and at the start of a cliff-walk with spectacular views. Walk the walk or surf the surf, and then come back for chowder, steak or fish in this very convivial bar. If you're tempted to stay for the session later on, there's a B&B behind the bar (Aughris House), also run by the McDermott family. En suite rooms, but fairly basic (€35pps).

By the Water's Edge | Coastal Retreats | 123

Ulster

Ulster | Co. Antrim

County Antrim

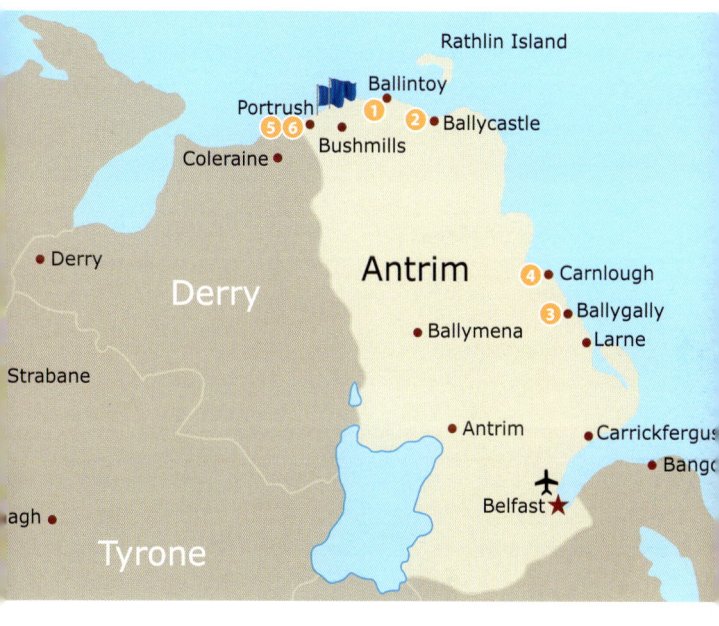

Introduction

At its narrowest, a channel of just 13 miles separates the coast of Antrim from Scotland. Starting in the more spectacular North Antrim, the Giant's Causeway (a World Heritage Site made up of some 40,000 basalt columns) looks like a massive set of stepping stones from sea to land, but is pleasantly accessible. The cliffs around it are breathtakingly high and breezy, but almost dwarfed by the 100-metre sheer drops off the western end of Rathlin Island. Below are pebbly beaches, with towering stacks of rock offshore. North Antrim has three Blue Flag beaches in Portrush and another at the friendly seaside town of Ballycastle. South Antrim is largely set around Belfast, and its most scenic spot is Islandmagee, a seven-metre-long peninsula with wild basalt cliffs, known as the Gobbins. To the east, the north-running coast from Larne is a series of spectacular and well-loved beaches.

By the Water's Edge | Coastal Retreats | 125

Ulster | Co. Antrim

Ulster | Co. Antrim

Left: The Giant's Causeway Above: Whitepark House, Ballintoy

Whitepark House

150 Whitepark Road, Ballintoy, Co. Antrim
T: 048 2073 1482 W: www.whiteparkhouse.com
Opening Times: Year round
Directions: *[Map Ref. 1] At Bushmills, take A2 to Whitepark Bay*

People only ever reach for superlatives after staying in Bob and Siobhan Isles' early-eighteenth-century house. It has that near-perfect blend of great location, beautiful decor, comfort, hospitality and value for money. There are three bedrooms (£50pps), all large, light and gorgeously furnished with antiques, ornate mirrors, four-poster beds and chaises longues. A path through the garden leads down to beautiful Whitepark Bay. Breakfast is served in the long, sunny conservatory, and delicious home-made cakes in the cosy sitting room. The whole house has a warm, sunny feeling. Bob's secret is probably that – unlike some who open their houses to guests – he genuinely enjoys playing host and being a guide to the area.

Ulster | Co. Antrim

Crockatinney Guesthouse
80 Whitepark Road, Ballycastle, Co. Antrim
T: 048 2076 8801 W: www.crockatinney.ndo.co.uk
Opening Times: Year round
Directions: *[Map Ref. 2] From Ballycastle, take Ballintoy road for 3 kilometres; just after sign for Kinbane Castle, at top of hill on left*
Fifteen minutes' drive from the Giant's Causeway, Crockatinney is a new, purpose-built guesthouse with stupendous views. It's built on elevated ground to overlook Ballycastle Bay, Fair Head, Rathlin Island and, on a clear day, the Mull of Kintyre. Ask for an upstairs room or you won't get the benefit of the view, though you will from the breakfast room. Rooms are no-frills but clean with good beds, and decent value at £30pps. Staff seem a little rushed, but are always willing to stop for a chat, or to point you in the right direction, should you wish to explore this stunning region.

Ballygally Castle Hotel
Coast Road, Ballygally, Co. Antrim
T: 048 2858 1066 W: www.hastingshotel.com
Opening Times: Mon-Sat 12.30pm-2.30pm and 5pm-9pm, Sun 12.30pm-2.30pm; bar and lounge lunch Mon-Sat 12.30pm-6pm, Sun 3.30pm-6pm
Directions: *[Map Ref. 3] On coast road (A2) between Larne and Glenarm*
The seventeenth-century Ballygally Castle forms the bulwark of the hotel – various extensions have been added over the centuries and fit in well. It's superbly located on the Antrim coast, with views over Ballygally Bay. Most rooms have been renovated to a good standard. The Antrim Suite has views to Fair Head, is very chic and – at £130pps – over twice the price of standard rooms. Rooms in the old castle are smaller and darker but atmospheric. Food can sometimes be hit or miss, but still the best in the area. One of them has been named the Ghost Room, and you may get a haunting. Good location, atmosphere, very friendly staff and some good deals (check website).

The Londonderry Arms
20 Harbour Road, Carnlough, Co. Antrim
T: 048 2888 5255 W: www.glensofantrim.com
Opening Times: Year round
Directions: *[Map Ref. 4] On main street, 14 miles from Larne*

Ulster | Co. Antrim

Ballygally Castle Hotel

In the glens of Antrim facing the sea, the Londonderry Arms has commendably avoided cashing in on the iconic status of its former owner by not renaming itself The Winston Churchill (he inherited the house through his great-grandmother, the Marchioness of Londonderry). He apparently used to stay in Room 114, which faces the sea and is a jazzed-up suite, but Room 116 is bigger and has a better view. Do ask for a suite (£67.50pps). The standard rooms (£55pps) mostly face the back and err towards old-fashioned. Food in the restaurant and bistro is good. The vibe here is relaxed and traditional, and manager Maureen Morrow is a welcoming host, but if you want five-star perfection, stay elsewhere.

Adelphi Portrush

67-71 Main Street, Portrush, Co. Antrim
T: 048 7082 5544 **W:** www.adelphiportrush.com
Opening Times: Bistro 8am-10am, noon-3pm and 5pm-9pm
Directions: *[Map Ref. 5] On Portrush Main Street*
The eco-credentials of this boutique hotel are impeccable – think state-of-the-art planning to ensure a tiny carbon footprint – and it's the best kind of family-run business. Mark and Amanda Holmes are attentive, dedicated hosts who welcome all suggestions/criticisms as helpful to improvement. Bedrooms are spacious and tasteful, with seaweed-extract toiletries in the bathrooms. It's in the centre of town, but five of the upper front bedrooms have Atlantic views.

Ulster | Co. Antrim

Food in the bistro is fresh, healthy and subtly flavoured, and there's a spa with underfloor heating. Portrush can be a bit manic; the Adelphi is an oasis. B&B £40-65pps and excellent family deals.

The Ramore Oriental Hotel

Harbour Road, Portrush, Co. Antrim
T: 048 7082 6969 W: www.ramorerestaurants.co.uk
Opening Times: Restaurant Wed-Thu 6pm-9.30pm, Fri-Sat 6pm-10pm, Sun 5.30pm-9.30pm
Directions: *[Map Ref. 6] On harbour in Portrush*

Portrush is a resort town with the usual promenades and games arcades, but it's also full of students from the nearby university, meaning it's buzzing all year round. Part of that buzz is definitely generated by George and Jane McAlpine's food empire along the harbour. They have three casual-dining places (the Wine Bar, the Harbour Bistro and Coast Restaurant) and one fine-dining restaurant, the Ramore Oriental. The old Ramore was one of the most famous restaurants in the North. This tries to continue that tradition, but has added Oriental to the title. So decide what you want to eat: for pasta/pizza, go to Coast; for bistro (e.g. prawns, garlic chicken, monkfish, etc.), go to the Wine Bar or the Harbour Bistro; and for fine Asian dining, go to the Ramore. All of them are lively and buzzy. The Ramore is the only one you can book – and make sure you do! For the others, join the queue, enjoy the prices and speed of delivery, and don't hold your breath waiting for your waiter to notice you.

Dunluce Castle

Ulster | Co.Derry

County Derry

Introduction

Northern Ireland's 200 kilometres of coast is in the care of the National Trust, and so carefully preserved and enhanced. Derry's finest beaches are to the north, where Portstewart Strand, with its two miles of golden sand and high dunes filled with wildflowers and butterflies, remains a strong and constant draw. At the east end of the beach, a picturesque World War II 'pillbox' remains, erected to deter an enemy invasion. The Barmouth, nearby, is a refuge for wildlife – waders and nesting birds – while the Mussenden Temple, commissioned by the Earl Bishop of Downhill and inspired by the Temple of Vesta in Tivoli, is architecturally compelling, and commands panoramic views across the Atlantic. Bangor Marina, nearby, is the North's largest marina and the setting for many sailing events, and Dundrum Bay has the glorious Tyrella Beach, with 25 hectares of mature, unspoiled dunes to explore.

Ulster | Co. Derry

Cul Erg

9 Hillside, Atlantic Circle, Portstewart, Co. Derry
T: 048 7083 6610 **W:** www.culerg.co.uk
Opening Times: Year round
Directions: *[Map Ref. 1] 2-minute walk from Portstewart Promenade; exit Portstewart towards Portrush, turn left into Atlantic Circle, bear left into Hillside, house on right*

Like the Victorians before them, families and surfers flock to this seaside town. The two miles of sandy beach are a huge draw. Cul Erg, a modern and popular B&B, is a two-minute walk from all the action on the old promenade. The interior is furnished to a high standard, with a coffee-and-cream colour scheme. The recently renovated dining room is particularly nice, with a row of windows on the ceiling to maximise light. Relax on one of the leather sofas in the family sitting room or tinkle at the piano. Bedrooms are spacious and immaculate, with cream-coloured soft furnishings, mahogany furniture, elegant throws and velvet cushions. En suite bathrooms have great showers. Most rooms to the front have sea views (B&B £40-50pps; £10 single supplement).

Golf course at Strand House, Portstewart

Ulster | Co.Derry

Sitting room at Strand House, Portstewart

Strand House

105 Strand Road, Portstewart, Co. Derry
T: 048 7083 1000 W: www.strandguesthouse.com
Opening Times: Year round
Directions: *[Map Ref. 2] From Portstewart head south on A2, take third exit on Diamond roundabout on to Strand Road; house on right*

As the name suggests, this stylish B&B enjoys an envious location overlooking Portstewart Strand, but it doesn't just depend on the view. It's great for golfers using the nearby links (a secure lock-room is provided for clubs and trolleys). The decor is decidedly chic – think Baileys liqueur and the occasional toffee hue. The lounge is full of natural light and minimal clutter, with a super-comfy couch. Don't ruin the beige carpet with sand-covered boots. Do borrow a book from their library. Bedrooms are a good size, with separate themes and great en suites. Some have jacuzzi baths, and there's a DVD player in each bedroom. Breakfasts are good, with home-made bread and organic fare, where possible. Request the Red Sails Room for a gorgeous sea view (B&B £60-120pps; 50% deposit required).

Ulster | Co.Derry

Ulster | Co. Donegal

County Donegal

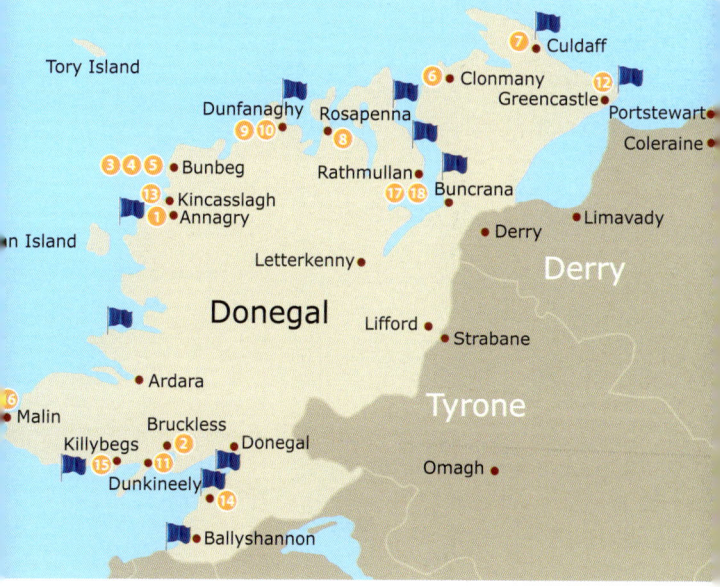

Introduction

The rugged, hollowed coastline of Donegal takes sharp, graphic turns through many spots of breathtaking beauty. Even though the roads closest to the shore are frequently poorly surfaced, they are worth the effort for the remarkable views they provide. To the south, Donegal Bay stretches from Bundoran to Donegal Town and on to Glencolmcille – all visible from the cliffs at Slieve League. The drive from Horn Head to Malin Head is a passage of pretty towns, villages and coastal wonders. Highlights are the sculpted rocks at Crohy Head, near Dungloe, the impressively named Bloody Foreland, and the panoramic seascapes around Horn Head and Rosguill. The section between Dungloe and Crolly is particularly rocky, but impressive nonetheless. Out to sea are Aran Island (Arranmore) and Tory Island to the north, where Balor, the Celtic god of darkness, is supposed to have lived on the eastern cliffs.

By the Water's Edge | Coastal Retreats

Ulster | Co. Donegal

Danny Minnie's Restaurant and B&B, Annagry

Danny Minnie's Restaurant and B&B

Annagry, Co. Donegal
T: 074 954 8201 **W:** www.dannyminnies.com
Opening Times: Closed Jan to mid-Feb, Sun throughout year (dinner only)
Directions: [Map Ref. 1] Annagry Village, R259 off N56

This place has been going nearly 50 years and is an institution. We're generally wary of 'institutions', but Danny Minnie's is an uplifting experience for the dining room alone: oak panelling, thick carpets, antiques, tapestries, brightly painted walls, candlelit tables – what a relief after that ubiquitous, Celtic Tiger frosty minimalism. Food (average €45-50 per person) is French-meets-Irish, *plus ou moins*, but can be a bit rich and heavy on the cream. Decor of the seven bedrooms is similarly quaint and olde worlde. Drambuie arrives with porridge in the morning. Nice touch. B&B €50-65pps.

Ulster | Co. Donegal

Bruckless House
Bruckless, Co. Donegal
T: 074 973 7071 W: www.bruckless.com
Opening Times: Closed Oct-31 Mar
Directions: *[Map Ref. 2] 12 miles west of Donegal, N56*
More cosy country house than the wilds of Donegal, Bruckless House is a listed Georgian building set in 18 acres of parkland, with award-winning gardens, a Connemara pony stud and direct access to Bruckless Bay. Joan and Clive Evans used to live in Hong Kong, and Chinese furniture is a feature of their elegant rooms. The four rooms (€65pps) – a twin, a double, and two singles sharing a bathroom – look out to the gardens. The highlight of breakfast: eggs from their own hens.

Ostán Gweedore
Bunbeg, Gweedore, Co. Donegal
T: 074 953 1177 W: www.ostangweedore.com
Opening Times: Feb-Nov; open for New Year
Directions: *[Map Ref. 3] R258 to Bunbeg*
A coastal guide can't overlook a place with one of the best views in the country, but make sure you get a room with a view across Gweedore Bay. About half the rooms have views (ask for 111-117). It can be noisy from time to time - this is a popular (and populist) wedding venue. The '70s architecture is matched by psychedelic carpeting inside, but don't let that put you off. Food, whether in the Ocean Restaurant (mains €26) or wine and tapas bar (dishes €6-22) is good quality – local products with an occasional hint of the Orient. B&B from €50pps. Save a few quid; keep an eye out for all manner of dinner deals and weekend breaks.

Teac Campbell
Bunbeg, Gweedore, Co. Donegal
T: 074 953 2270 W: www.teac-campbell.com
Opening Times: Year round
Directions: *[Map Ref. 4] R258 to Bunbeg*
Charlie and Máire Campbell have been running this popular guesthouse for years, and it's surprising Bord Fáilte doesn't dispatch fledging hoteliers to learn the secret of hospitality from them. They welcome you with tea, phone restaurants to check availability, advise on pubs and outings, chat as long as you like, and make a fuss of your kids. The ivy-clad house is attractive, with

Ulster | Co. Donegal

photos, drawings and historical memorabilia throughout the rooms, and the location is superb. Eight rooms at the back have views of the Atlantic. B&B €35-37.50pps, and less for triple rooms.

Teach Beag Hudí
Bunbeg Harbour, Gweedore, Co. Donegal
T: 074 953 1016
Opening Times: Year round
Directions: *[Map Ref. 5] Turn off from R257 towards port*
This used to be the kind of small, smoky pub you'd spend hours in, losing track of time. Now the smokers are all outside, but it still hosts one of the best trad sessions round every Monday evening, and a smaller one on Friday. Owned by Proinsias Ó Maonaigh, father of Altan's Mairéad Ní Mhaonaigh, expect to hear all kinds of instruments – mandolins, whistles, accordions – and all kinds of players, from Japan, Canada and the next village …

Glen House €
Clonmany, Ballyliffin, Co. Donegal
T: 074 937 6745 W: www.glenhouse.ie
Opening Times: Year round; restaurant by appointment only, dinner Tue-Sun (peak season)/Thu-Sun (off-season), lunch Sun only
Directions: *[Map Ref. 6] R238 from Buncrana, through Clonmany*
This spacious Georgian house with sweeping sea views, and a conservatory looking on to Glenevin Waterfall is close to Ballyliffin golf course, and a good base for exploring Inishowen Peninsula. They'll cook you dinner on request, and Sunday lunch is fantastic value at €16.95. Ask for one of the two first-floor front rooms looking out to sea – only €5 more than standard rooms and worth it. B&B €40-55pps.

McGrory's of Culdaff
Culdaff, Inishowen Peninsula, Co. Donegal
T: 074 937 9104 W: www.mcgrorys.ie
Opening Times: Year round; restaurant closed Mon
Directions: *[Map Ref. 7] R238 around Inishowen Peninsula*
Near the northernmost tip of Ireland, in an isolated area (though recently filling with holiday homes), and after over 80 years in business, McGrory's maintains and exceeds its own high standards, with nonchalant ease. We're quite in awe of this family. If you're on the Inishowen Peninsula, you'll definitely come here, and chances

Ulster | Co. Donegal

are you made the trek especially to hear a session in the Backroom (anyone from Republic of Loose to Arlo Guthrie), sample mussels in the Front Bar or wild salmon (€28) in the restaurant, and, finally, retire to an impeccably clean and cheerful room upstairs (B&B €40-70pps).

Rosapenna Hotel and Golf Resort

Downings, Co. Donegal
T: 074 915 5301 W:
www.rosapenna.ie
Opening Times: Closed end Oct-St. Patrick's Day
Directions: *[Map Ref. 8] N56, then R245 to Carrickart, 2.5 kilometres farther*

The name rather gives it away. If you're a golfer, do you need our recommendation to stay here? If you're not, will you want to stay? Non-golfers may have to put up with constant conversations about the 'difficult approach on the fifth', or the 'challenging back nine', but there's a pool, tennis, snooker, decent food, and two beaches close by to offer a worthwhile distraction. The rooms, lounges and restaurant make the most of the location on Sheephaven Bay. Forty of the rooms have sea views – ask for the bay-view suites for magnificent views and big balconies. B&B from €85pps and excellent reductions on green fees (obviously!).

Old Tom at Rosapenna Hotel and Golf Resort

The Cove

Port na Blagh, Dunfanaghy, Co. Donegal
T: 074 913 6399
Opening Times: Closed Mon and Jan-St. Patrick's Day
Directions: *[Map Ref. 9] Port na Blagh, overlooking harbour, on N56*

Ulster | Co. Donegal

Small and popular, so even if you book, you'll probably have to wait for a table, but you'll be taken to the first-floor bar with views over the harbour, so no hardship. Dining is downstairs – no view, but a roaring fire and surprisingly good art on the walls. Start with the chowder (€7.50) or whole boned quail (€9.50) and move on to monkfish (€24) or pork belly (€19.50). The early-bird three-course set dinner is good value at €25.

Shandon Hotel Spa and Fitness

Marble Hill Strand, Port na Blagh, Dunfanaghy, Co. Donegal
T: 074 913 6137 W: www.shandonhotel.com
Opening Times: Closed Nov to mid-Mar
Directions: *[Map Ref. 10] N56 to Dunfanaghy*
This family favourite has a hint of Butlins' atmosphere, perhaps because of the '70s decor, the kids' club and the range of activities: horse-riding, snooker, football, tennis, basketball, etc. But we won't hold that against it. Enjoy the spectacular views – all 50 rooms face Sheephaven Bay – and paddle in the lovely beach or soak in the spa (newly built and very 'noughties'). Food is decent, especially the substantial breakfast. From €75pps. All kinds of deals and kids' rates.

Castle Murray House Hotel, St. John's Point, Dunkineely

Ulster | Co. Donegal

Castle Murray House Hotel
St. John's Point, Dunkineely, Co. Donegal
T: 074 973 7022 W: www.castlemurray.com
Opening Times: Closed mid-Jan to mid-Feb
Directions: *[Map Ref. 11]* N56, first left outside Dunkineely Village

Small, friendly, fantastic views, great food, and good value ... Castle Murray House has a lot of faithful customers. Just ten rooms – nine have sea views on St. John's Point, but try for the Ballysaggart Room, which has a balcony and full-on view (all rooms are identically priced, from €65pps). The restaurant looks out to the ruins of fifteenth-century Rahan's Castle by the sea, and chef Remy Dupuy produces delicious, simple French cooking with local ingredients. There's seafood, game in winter, and great vegetarian options, like aubergine ravioli with chickpeas. Set menu €51.

Kealy's Seafood Bar
Greencastle, Co. Donegal
T: 074 938 1010 E: kealysseafoodbar@yahoo.ie
Opening Times: Closed Mon-Tue; dinner Wed-Sun, lunch Fri-Sun
Directions: *[Map Ref. 12]* On harbour at Greencastle

This is the kind of unpretentious spot that gets foodies drooling. The exterior is misleading - it could almost be a chippie. Food is classic-imaginative: hake in saffron sauce, plaice in anchovy butter, baked salmon with wholegrain mustard. Tricia Kealy's chowder and home-baked breads are famous. The place is always full of holidaymakers who've popped over from Derry and appreciate value. Set dinner menu €40.

Iggy's Bar
Kincasslagh, Co. Donegal
T: 074 954 3112
Opening Times: No food Sun; food served noon-6pm in summer
Directions: *[Map Ref. 13]* Kincasslagh Main Street; on corner, turn for harbour

Ann Murray, Iggy's wife, cooks the chowder, mussels, lobster, turbot and prawns that keep bringing people back to the only pub in this tiny seaside village. The produce is straight in from the harbour. The dish of the day depends on what's caught and Ann's mood. Take whatever's on offer. It's all good and great value – average price is €12 per dish. This is Stephen Rea's (and a lot of other, less-famous people's) favourite pub. Daniel O'Donnell was born here (in Kincasslagh – not Iggy's).

By the Water's Edge | Coastal Retreats | **141**

Ulster | Co. Donegal

Coxtown Manor
Laghey, Co. Donegal
T: 074 973 4575 W: www.coxtownmanor.com
Opening Times: Closed Nov and 6 Jan-6 Feb; restaurant closed Sun-Mon
Directions: [Map Ref. 14] Off N15 between Ballyshannon and Donegal Town

Admittedly, this is located more in rolling hills than right on the coast, but it's close enough to Donegal Bay to count, and we wouldn't want pedantry to keep you from this attractive guesthouse. Sadly, dinner is no longer on offer, which does lessen its charms somewhat. The whole point of coming here was that you never had to leave – food, drink, scenery and ambience were at your fingertips – but they still do snacks like sandwiches, soups, salads and the famous Belgian chocolate mousse, and the bar is open till midnight, complete with Belgian beers. (Owner Edward Dewael is from guess-which-country.) Breakfast offers eggs from their own hens, and Mediterranean tomato and cucumber salad. B&B price has gone down since the restaurant closed. €50-70pps.

Kitty Kelly's
Largy, Killybegs, Co. Donegal
T: 074 973 1925 W: www.kittykellys.com
Opening Times: Closed Nov-Feb
Directions: [Map Ref. 15] 5 kilometres west of Killybegs, on coast road to Kilcar

The decor in this 200-year-old, fuchsia-painted farmhouse just beyond Killybegs is cosy, cluttered and rustic – wooden floors, low ceilings, stone walls, dressers, lots of prints. The menu is extensive. The oysters grilled with bacon and cheddar is perfectly appetising, but go for the catch of the day, especially when it's mackerel (too few restaurants serve mackerel, which, when fresh, is unbeatable) or orange roughy (€19.95), a 'new' meaty, sustainable fish.

Malin Hotel
Malin, Co. Donegal
T: 074 937 0606 W: www.malinhead.ie
Opening Times: Year round
Directions: [Map Ref. 16] Malin Town, overlooking the green

Congratulations! You've reached the country's most northerly tip,

Ulster | Co. Donegal

Innisfree Bay, Co. Donegal

and very beautiful and windswept it is, too. For luxury and protection against the wild Atlantic, stay in the Malin Hotel. It may look a bit sprawling – all extension and no house – but inside it's incongruously plush (four-poster beds, Egyptian cotton sheets, Monsoon showers, complimentary chocolates). Consistently excellent staff under manager John Keyes and a good, strong menu (scallops €7.95, John Dory with tomato pesto €22.95) ensure a happy stay. The best rooms overlook the village green. B&B from €55pps.

Fort Royal
Rathmullan, Co. Donegal
T: 074 915 8100 W: www.fortroyalhotel.com
Opening Times: Closed 1 Nov-7 Apr
Directions: *[Map Ref. 17] R247 from Ramelton, 1/4 mile beyond Rathmullan Village*
You won't get a better location than Tim and Tina Fletcher's comfortable, spacious Victorian house, set on 19 acres above Lough Swilly. A track winds through the grounds to a safe and sandy beach; there's tennis, pitch 'n' putt and an arboretum. Staying here feels like somewhere between a guesthouse and hotel with great amenities, and is good value at €65-75pps. Dinner (€45 menu Mon-Sat, residents only) uses home-grown vegetables and local produce. Desserts are especially good.

Ulster | Co. Donegal

Rathmullan House

Rathmullan, Co. Donegal
T: 074 915 8188 W: www.rathmullanhouse.com
Opening Times: Closed early Jan to mid-Feb
Directions: *[Map Ref. 18] R247 from Ramelton, through Rathmullan Village and turn right*

River Café's Rose Gray was here this March to cook with head chef Ian Orr – a signal, if you hadn't already worked it out, that Rathmullan House is a serious destination for foodies. The dining room was designed by Liam McCormick, who is more famous for designing churches, but then, eating here is a religion for some people. The food is traditional-contemporary (roast venison served pink). Set menus €45 and €55. A great feature is the children's menu – not the usual sausages and chips, but a condensed version of adult fare. In its own grounds, on the shores of Lough Swilly, this former Georgian summer-house is now run by the energetic Wheeler brothers and their wives, and this lot do not rest on their laurels – last year they put on *The Tempest* in the new open-air theatre. The best sea views are in rooms 4 and 6; some of the rooms in the new Regency Wing have glimpses of the sea, but in summer, the foliage grows high. B&B from €80pps, but can be twice that for the best rooms in high season. All the rooms are attractive, but do vary in terms of decor, size and view, so it's worth being specific when you book.

Rathmullan House

Ulster | Co. Down

County Down

Introduction

Down's rocky coastline is spanned by Belfast Lough, in the north, and Carlingford Lough, in the south – just on the border with Co. Louth and, in the words of the old Percy French song, 'where the mountains of Mourne sweep down to the sea'. Indeed, from the top of Slieve Donard, the highest mountain in the Mourne range (2,785 feet, for those of an adventurous disposition), they say you can make out Belfast to the north and Dublin to the south on a clear day – if you can take your eyes off the breathtaking views of the coastline below. Strangford Lough, which dominates the eastern seaboard of the county, isn't technically a 'lough' – the Ards Peninsula stretches right round in an arc from Bangor to Downpatrick (where, they say, St. Patrick is buried), where a small isthmus separates it from the mainland. There are several islands off the coast, including New Island, the Copeland Islands and Canon Rock, the country's easternmost point.

By the Water's Edge | Coastal Retreats | 145

Ulster | Co. Down

Cairn Bay Lodge, Bangor

Cairn Bay Lodge €
278 Seacliff Road, Bangor, Co. Down
T: 048 9146 7636 **W:** www.cairnbaylodge.com
Opening Times: Year round
Directions: *[Map Ref. 1] Outskirts of Bangor, in Ballyholme*
This Edwardian villa overlooking Ballyholme Bay scores high for hospitality and style. Rooms are graceful and smartly finished, with period furniture. Breakfast includes baked goat's cheese with tomato, smoked-salmon omelette and, of course, the Ulster fry. Chris and Jenny Mullen strike a good balance between warmth and reserve (the family atmosphere of a B&B meets the discretion of a guesthouse). Jenny is also a qualified beauty therapist, and will

Ulster | Co. Down

provide on-site treatments. B&B £35-40pps. Just three rooms. Ask for the Ballyholme Room, overlooking the bay.

Jeffers by the Marina
7 Gray's Hill, Bangor, Co. Down
T: 048 9185 9555 W: www.jeffersbythemarina.com
Opening Times: Closed Mon
Directions: *[Map Ref. 2] Bangor, overlooking marina*
Definitely come for breakfast, and choose from a very extensive menu: there are free-range eggs and potato bread with the 'Big Breakfast' (£7.50). For lunch, try the wild venison burger (£9.50); for dinner, there's fish, chicken, beef and pork belly. Enjoy the relaxed, no-nonsense, timeless harbourside decor and the confident, tasty cooking. Raise your voice to be heard over the clatter of other diners.

Royal Hotel
26-28 Quay Street, Bangor, Co. Down
T: 048 9127 1866 W: www.the-royal-hotel.com
Opening Times: Year round
Directions: *[Map Ref. 3] Bangor, facing marina; turn right on Main Street*
This large red-brick Victorian hotel, overlooking Bangor's marina, is still family run and has an endearing charm. Recent renovations have improved many of the rooms, but they still vary in size and quality. The 24 front rooms are sea-facing. You could nitpick that the place remains in need of upgrading and the marina can be a noisy place, but the Royal is an institution, rates are reasonable, and we like its easy-going seaside-resort charm. B&B from £40pps.

The Carriage House
71 Main Street, Dundrum, Co. Down
T: 048 4375 1635 W: www.carriagehousedundrum.com
Opening Times: Daily in summer; phone for off-season opening times
Directions: *[Map Ref. 4] Dundrum, across from harbour*
Right across from the harbour, Maureen Griffith's bright blue house can't be missed. Inside, the eclecticism and forceful artistic personality that chose those blue walls is much in evidence: there are antiques, *objets d'art*, prints, paintings and contemporary pieces, including a life-size sculpture of a horse out back, and quite

Ulster | Co. Down

a menagerie of pets, including (on our last visit) a hedgehog. There are three rooms to choose from, two with views of Murlough Bay. Flowers in the rooms and fresh linen on the king-size beds assure your comfort. B&B £35pps.

Mourne's Seafood Bar €
10 Main Street, Dundrum, Co. Down
T: 048 4375 1377 W: www.mourneseafood.com
Opening Times: Closed Mon off-season
Directions: *[Map Ref. 5] Main Street, Dundrum*

This tiny town, at the foot of the Mourne Mountains, is spawning an empire that started in this bar. Joanne and Robert McCoubrey now have a Mourne's Seafood Bar in Belfast and a Mourne Café in nearby Newcastle – and they run boat tours along the Mourne coast. Busy, busy, busy. Can they maintain standards? Judging by our last visit, yes. The food remains simple, tasty and well priced (starters about £5, mains £12.50). Being eco-conscious, they use sustainable, local fish, like gurnard and ling, and their shellfish is from their own beds in Carlingford Lough. Seafood means seafood, but there's rib-eye steak for the hardened carnivores.

Seasalt Delicatessen and Bistro €
51 Central Promenade, Newcastle, Co. Down
T: 048 4372 5027 W: www.seasaltnewcastle.co.uk
Opening Times: Daily in summer; phone for off-season hours
Directions: *[Map Ref. 6] Newcastle, on seafront*

Newcastle can be chintzy, but Aidan Small's airy little bistro and delicatessen, right on the seafront, is suitably chic. He does truly excellent sandwiches (roast beef and horseradish, pastrami and smoked cheese, both £3.50), a trademark chowder (£3.95) and great evening tapas, which you can enjoy while watching the waves outside. Ranging in price from £2.25 (olives) to £4.95 (fillet-steak strips), these tapas are delicious little things. Four or five should fill you up.

Slieve Donard Resort and Spa
Newcastle, Co. Down
T: 048 4372 1066 W: www.hastingshotel.com
Opening Times: Year round
Directions: *[Map Ref. 7] 30 miles south of Belfast on A24*

This magnificent, majestic and – dare we say it – slightly kitsch late-

Ulster | Co. Down

Slieve Donard Resort and Spa, Newcastle

Victorian building, standing on its own acreage beneath the Mourne Mountains, will definitely impress. The vast white chandeliered reception sets the tone; the spa is pretty amazing, and pretty pricey, but no one swimming in the pool with floor-to-ceiling views of mountains and sea would grudge a penny. You might, after all this opulence, be disappointed by the size of your standard room (£80pps), but not if you have a new resort suite (£235pps). The Hastings Hotel Group took over Slieve Donard in 1972 (it was previously built and owned by the Great Northern Railway) and turned it into a luxury brand, with all the trimmings. A popular wedding venue in the summer, meaning it can get crowded, but that's better than it being empty, right? Their standards are high, they have a lot to offer, and work at going that extra yard to justify their prices.

Villa Vinci €

31 Main Street, Newcastle, Co. Down
T: 048 4372 3080
Opening Times: Year round
Directions: *[Map Ref. 8] Main Street, Newcastle*
Everyone likes Villa Vinci's simple, strong Mediterranean cooking. After all these seafood restaurants, we're delighted to be recommending this Italian restaurant. The light, airy, contemporary

Ulster | Co. Down

decor and friendly service make it a pleasant place to sit, and it does excellent (and excellent-value) soups, pastas, steaks, seafood, salads and desserts. Try the prawn cocktail, an excellent revisiting of the '70s classic.

The Whistledown Hotel

6 Seaview, Warrenpoint, Co. Down
T: 048 4175 4174 W: www.thewhistledownhotel.com
Opening Times: Year round
Directions: *[Map Ref. 9] Warrenpoint, on seafront*

They are very fond of red at The Whistledown: red walls in the bar, red benches in the bistro, and red cushions, blankets, valences and sofas in the bedroom. We're seeing red, but red in a warm bolero way – not red-angry. Staff are great, the showers are power, the decor is half chic/half nuts, the food is really very good. It's a corner hotel. The presidential and bridal suites face Carlingford Lough (and, at £75pps, are just £15 more than standard rooms). The remainder of the 22 rooms face the Mourne Mountains. We like this place. It's right on the border and price comparisons – Sunday lunch for £16.95 – do us down South few favours. Our finance minister says it's unpatriotic of us to shop up North, but hell, Mr Minister, that makes us see red ...

Ulster | Co. Down

Resorts Index | A–Z

A

Abbey Tavern, Dublin	16
Achill Cliff House Hotel, Mayo	116
Adelphi Portrush, Antrim	129
Admiralty Lodge, Clare	51
Aldridge Lodge, Wexford	32
An Dún, Galway	100
An Fulacht Fia, Clare	42
Anglers Return, The; Galway	110
An Leath Phingin Eile, Kerry	82
Annie's Restaurant, Cork	55
Aqua, Dublin	17
Aran Islands Hotel, Galway	101
Aran View House Hotel, Clare	43
Ardagh Hotel and Restaurant, Galway	107
Ardmore Country House, Mayo	118
Ashe's Seafood Bar and B&B, Kerry	77

B

Backstage@Bel's, Wicklow	37
Ballinalacken Castle, Clare	44
Ballintaggart House, Kerry	78
Ballygally Castle Hotel, Antrim	128
Ballylickey House, Cork	56
Barrtra Seafood Restaurant, Clare	48
Bayview Hotel, Cork	54
Beach Bar, The/Aughris House, Sligo	123
Beach Guesthouse, Waterford	96
Beehive, The; Mayo	116
Bella Vista Bar and Bistro, Sligo	123
Bervie, The; Mayo	117
Blairs Cove House, Cork	56
Blue Haven Hotel, Cork	66
Bon Appétit, Dublin	18
Brook Lane Hotel, Kerry	83
Bruckless House, Donegal	137
Burren Coast Hotel, Clare	42
Butler Arms, Kerry	89

C

Cabot's Source@The Linen Mill, Mayo	119
Cairbre House, Waterford	94
Cairn Bay Lodge, Down	146
Carriage House, The; Down	147
Casey's of Baltimore, Cork	55
Casino House, Cork	65
Castle Murray House Hotel, Donegal	141
Castleview Heights Restaurant, Wexford	31
Castlewood House, Kerry	79
Cavistons, Dublin	16
Chart House, The; Kerry	79
Cliff House Hotel, The; Waterford	92
Connemara Coast Hotel, Galway	111
Cornerstone, The; Clare	48
Cove, The; Donegal	139
Coxtown Manor, Donegal	142
Crockatinney Guesthouse, Antrim	128
Cronin's Pub, Cork	63
Cronin's Sheebeen, Mayo	119
Cul Erg, Derry	132
Cullinan's, Clare	45

D

Danny Minnie's, Donegal	136
D'Arcy's, Kerry	84
Deasy's Harbour Bar, Cork	59
Derrynane Hotel and Restaurant, Kerry	75
Derrynane House Tea Rooms, Kerry	76
Dingle Skellig Hotel, Kerry	80
Diva Restaurant and Piano Bar, Wicklow	37
Dolphin Beach House, Galway	108
Dolphin Hotel and Restaurant, Galway	112
Doolin Café, The; Clare	45
Doonmore Hotel, Galway	113
Dunbrody Country House Hotel, Wexford	29

F

Finnegan's, Dublin	14
Fisherman's Cottage, Galway	101
Fishy Fishy Café, Cork	66

152 | By the Water's Edge | Coastal Retreats